Praise for

The Wise Planner

"Whether it's a will or trust, Terry takes the most complex estate and tax planning strategies and makes them easy for anyone to understand. … with Terry's wise and comforting counsel you can not only help yourself and your family plan for the future, but create the legacy you desire. Most of us spend more time planning for our vacations. Spend a little time with Terry's guidebook, and you'll plan for the most important destination of your life … your family's future."

> — Scott James, Senior Vice President, Regional Manager,
> *Wells Fargo Wealth Management Group*

"Terry Kane has succeeded in putting a relaxed, conversational tone to an oft-avoided subject, in language anyone can understand. ... This book is a quick and entertaining read, yet informs on nearly every subject your lawyer, your banker, and your wealth management advisor should be talking to you about. Aspiring financial advisors, bankers, financial planners, CPAs and lawyers will also learn from Terry's writing style and wit."

> — David Spence, Estate Planning and Tax Attorney,
> *Royse Law Firm*

"An excellent book, great practical advice well organized and easy to read. I loved the quotes."

> — Honorable John A. Flaherty (Ret.), *JAMS*

"Many times during my years of law practice I have wished there was a book on estate planning and family wealth preservation that I could heartily recommend to clients and friends. Not so they wouldn't have to ask me for advice, but so that when they did seek advice they were better informed and more focused. Terry Kane's *The Wise Planner* is just the book. It is wise and witty. It contains clearly written, easy-to-understand explanations of tax and estate planning issues, and it is loaded with sound practical advice. And don't miss the chapter

on scams. *The Wise Planner* will have a prominent place on my recommended reading list for clients, friends and my own family!"
> — Filmore Rose, Estate Planning and Tax Attorney,
>   Of Counsel to *Lane Powell*

"Terry Kane has done a marvelous job of introducing the complex issues of wealth preservation and management. In the manner of a fine teacher, he exposes the elements that a layperson needs to know to work constructively with his or her financial advisors."
> — Joseph H. Moless, Jr., Dean, *Lincoln Law School*

"The discussion of GRATs, FLPs and Charitable Trusts is very well done. It covers a very complex area in a way which should be quite understandable to the average person. ... A fine book which gives valuable information..."
> — Francis B. Doyle, Estate Planning and Tax Attorney,
>   *WealthPLAN*

"Recently, I began serving as trustee of a family trust, and from that experience, I found the information in Terry's book invaluable for people setting up a trust or serving as trustees. I'm giving copies to my friends and family."
> — Suzanne Childs, *Attorney*

"*The Wise Planner* is a great guide to estate planning. Terry provides a simple, easy approach in understanding this process."
> — Jack Wong, Senior Vice President, Senior Financial
>   Consultant, *Wells Fargo Investment LLC, Private Client
>   Services*

The Wise Planner: Safeguarding Your Family's Wealth

Terry Kane,
M.Phil, J.D.

WISEGUY
PRESS

The Wise Planner: Safeguarding Your Family's Wealth

Copyright © 2009 by Terence M. Kane. All rights reserved.

Library of Congress Control Number: 2009932142

Published by WiseGuy Press, Inc., San Jose, CA 95150

Find us on the Web at www.WiseGuyPress.com

WiseGuy Press also publishes its books in a variety of electronic formats. For more information about WiseGuy Press products, visit our website at www.WiseGuyPress.com.

WiseGuy Press is a registered trademark (pending) of WiseGuy Press, Incorporated in the United States.

Editor: Judy Kane
Cover by: Barbara Oertli Design
Proofreaders: Holly Kane and Mary Kane

ISBN: 978-0-9841361-0-0
10 9 8 7 6 5 4 3 2 1

Printed and bound in the United States of America

This book is dedicated to my family:
Mary, the clean-up reader,
Holly, the authoritarian grammarian,
and especially to my wife, Judy,
with admiration, appreciation, and greatest affection.

Table of Contents

Table of Contents

♦ "The manner of giving is worth more ..."
Pierre Corneille

♦ "Death is not the worst evil ..."
Attr. to Sophocles

♦ "I don't want to achieve immortality ..."
Attr. to   Leo Durocher

♦ "Live honestly, eat slowly ..."
Lucille Ball

♦ "We know now that we can't beat their machines. ..."
Gene Barry as Dr. Clayton Forrester

♦ "I hope that we shall crush ..."
Thomas Jefferson

♦ "The limited liability corporation is the greatest ..."
Nicholas Murray Butler

Table of Contents

Chapter Contents: Avoiding Litigation ▶ Alternatives to Litigation ▶ Alternative Dispute Resolution ▶ Mediation ▶ Arbitration ▶ How to Deal With People Who Owe You Money ▶ Understanding Workouts ▶ Using Available Information Wisely ▶ Bankruptcy and You

♦ "Discourage litigation ..."
   Abraham Lincoln

♦ "I don't know as I want a lawyer telling me ..."
   J P Morgan

Scams, and How To Avoid Them

Chapter Content: Internet Based Scams ▶ You Have Already Won! ▶ Pyramids and Condominiums ▶ The False Balance Sheet and Tax Return ▶ No Taxes Ever! ▶ The Private Annuity Trust or PAT

♦ "The secret to life is honesty and fair dealing ..."
   Groucho Marx

♦ "It is easy at any moment to surrender ..."
   Titus Livius (Livy)

INTRODUCTION

Having control is important. No one wants to be at the mercy of the system, especially when it comes to safeguarding their family's wealth. Yet many people have little or no idea about how to minimize the financial risks in their lives. This book is designed to change that.

How can you protect you family's assets? Can you keep your personal assets separate from your business liabilities by incorporating? Do you need an estate plan to protect your family? Is it better to go to a lawyer and hope that he or she will take good care of you, or should you do it yourself with self-help books? Is cheaper to do it on your own?

Drafting your own legal documents is complex and boring. Even more importantly, when you're done you still won't know if you've gotten it right. You won't know if the do-it-yourself plan you're working from is up to date and current. And you don't know if it applies to your family, your goals and your life.

If you choose to work with an attorney, you'll need to have information that will help you make sound legal and financial decisions. You'll need knowledge that's up to date and current, about your own situation and about the various ways you can safeguard your wealth.

By using this book, you'll gain the information and knowledge you need to make the best use of your time. You'll be aware of options and potential opportunities to avoid legal, tax and financial risks. And when you meet with your legal and financial advisors you'll be prepared to ask the right questions, and you'll understand the reasons behind the answers. You'll no longer be blindly following the ideas and methods suggested by others. Instead, you'll understand strategies that actually fit your values, your family situation, your attitudes and your plans. As a result, you'll play an active role in creating a plan that's right for you.

You'll be in control of safeguarding your family's wealth.

PART I: ESTATE PLANNING AND WEALTH PRESERVATION

"Planning is half the battle.
Surprise is half the battle.
Being prepared is half the battle.
Lots of things are half the battle."

Kevin Costner as Elliot Ness, The
Untouchables (1990)

Everyone says that you need a plan to preserve your wealth and to protect your estate, but no one explains exactly why, or what a plan does for you. In a nutshell, a good plan will protect the money and assets you've spent your life earning from estate taxes and probate costs and fees. With a good plan, you'll know your family is protected and your wealth has been preserved.

CHAPTER 1:

The Pirate's Warning: Nobody Gets Out Alive!

Chapter Contents: What's In This Book ▶ How the Information is Organized ▶ Avoiding Legal Risks: My Disclaimer ▶ Why Read This Book?

A tombstone on the Isla Mujeres, off Mexico's eastern coast, was erected for the 18th century pirate and slave trader Fermin Mundaca. The dead man's words, inscribed on it, speak simply and directly to the living who stand before it:

> "As you are, I once was.
> As I am, you will be."

And if mortality isn't enough of a problem, Ben Franklin had a warning of his own:

> "... in this world nothing is certain but death and taxes."
> Benjamin Franklin (1706–1790)

Unless the world is a lot different for you than for the rest of the human race, two things are certain: you're going to die, and you're going to pay taxes.

What's in This Book. The world is full of risks. This book is about planning that will help you understand and minimize these risks. This isn't an exercise about contemplating disaster and death or trying to make your heirs happy after you're gone. It's about you, and your happiness. You can be in control of your financial future and feel secure, even in uncertain times.

America's tax laws are undergoing some of the most significant changes in decades. By the time you've finished this book, you'll know what has changed, what may change, and what may change again. I'll give you practical advice and information about probate, civil, tax, and bankruptcy laws that you need to understand to protect yourself, your family, and your business.

How the Information is Organized. This book has three main segments. First, you need to understand some basics about three related topics: asset management, wealth preservation and estate planning.

- Asset management is minimizing risk and maximizing control over your investments;
- Wealth preservation is keeping your investments intact and growing safely;
- Estate planning is passing wealth safely to your heirs according to your wishes.

Whether your plans are basic or sophisticated depends on your needs and preferences. If you plan poorly, or don't plan at all, your survivors will pay tens of thousands of dollars in probate fees, experience time delays averaging a year to a year and a half, and may pay twice as much in estate taxes as someone with a complete and up to date estate plan!

Second, we'll consider advanced planning techniques. There's practical information on powers of attorney for finances and for health care, and the whole alphabet soup of modern planning ideas, like CRATs and GRATs, QPRTs and ILITs.

Third, we'll deal with other civil and tax problems. You can use litigation avoidance strategies, including formation of business entities like corporations and LLC's to avoid costly and dangerous liability traps. I'll include brief discussions of principles from bankruptcy law, and some advice on how to deal with businesses or individuals that owe you money. I'll also explain some other strategies to avoid financial threats and scams, and how to avoid other dangerous and costly mistakes.

In the course of our time together I hope to scare you, amuse you, and inform you. I know you need real, solid information, and I'm going to give you plenty. I will tell you frightening facts about the dangerous legal and practical problems we're trying to prevent using factual details that have been edited so you can't recognize or trace any of the people involved. However, other than some name changes to protect the innocent (or semi-innocent), these situations are real, not hypothetical. The advice I'm giving you, although lighthearted in presentation, is very serious.

Avoiding Legal Risks: My Disclaimer. Everything comes with a disclaimer these days. This book does, too. In the Maltese Falcon, Humphrey Bogart, as hard-boiled detective Sam Spade, is talking to the District Attorney. According to the D.A., even if Spade isn't certain who killed his partner, he must have a pretty good guess. Bogart fires back:

"My guess might be excellent, or it might be crummy, but Mrs. Spade didn't raise any children dippy enough to make guesses in front of a District Attorney, an assistant District Attorney, and a stenographer...."

[aside to the stenographer] "You getting this all right, son, or am I going too fast for you?"

Mrs. Kane, my mother, didn't raise any children dippy enough to promise that the answers to all of the world's complex legal questions are guaranteed to be here in a one-size-fits-all format.

Buying this book or any other book doesn't give you a license to practice law. Most parts of the legal system, especially estate and tax planning, take years of study and training to understand. Although some bits of advice in this book will be straightforward enough that you might want to do it yourself and save a few bucks, most of what's here is complex. It deals with the most important financial and legal decisions you are faced with and shouldn't be implemented without a lawyer's help. You have better things to do with your time than spend years of work and study just so you can prepare the documents for your own estate or asset protection plan.

Why Read This Book? Knowledge is power, and learning about these strategies and tools will give you power. Having this power is especially important because you'll be dealing with attorneys and accountants when you implement your plan.

Organizing your thoughts and your ideas about your estate plan is very important. You need to know what you want to do with your property, what your heirs and beneficiaries may expect or need, and gather this information together. This, coupled with the knowledge you'll have about planning, will give you an essential leg up.

Instead of learning about problems and solutions when you first meet with your professional advisors, you'll already be armed with information. Your attorney's role, for example, is helping you document and create the plan that will accomplish your goals. If you know what you want to accomplish before you meet with your attorney, you'll be an informed client. You'll get better results faster, and since attorneys often charge by the hour, for less money. You, your attorney, and your other advisors, will choose and implement the right strategies to minimize financial and tax risks for you and your family. And you'll do it with confidence.

CHAPTER 2:

Basic Planning

Chapter Contents: Why You Must Plan Now ▸ Personalized Planning is the Only Successful Planning ▸ Wealth Planning ▸ Modern Portfolio Theory and Asset Allocation

New Lesson From an Old Story: David and Goliath. If you're like me, the likely outcome to the story of David and Goliath seemed obvious. Goliath was a towering giant, an oversized killing machine, with the weapons and armor of a professional soldier. David was a little shepherd boy, armed only with a slingshot. But David was the hero of the story. As my dad used to say, the smart money wasn't betting on Goliath. Nevertheless, I did find a surprise in the story. While David was preparing for the fight, he went to the stream bed and selected "five smooth stones."

Five smooth stones? David was a biblical hero with divine backing! He even killed Goliath on the first shot... but he still took extra ammo! I imagine him talking to another shepherd as he's poking around that stream bed before the fight, filling his pocket with rocks: "The Lord is mighty, and will protect me... But have you seen the size of that Goliath guy?"

The Lesson: Contingency planning is good for everyone. This holds true even if some of the contingencies never occur. Time spent planning for eventualities that don't occur isn't time wasted, it's an investment in peace of mind.

Why You Must Plan Now. Isn't now a bad time to plan? The tax laws are changing in several important ways. No one is certain whether further changes will happen, or what form those changes will take. Wouldn't a sensible person postpone making plans right now?

The truth is just the opposite. Now is the essential time to plan. How you hold your family's wealth is important for your protection and peace of mind. How it transitions to the next generation is crucial. I'll lay out the context you need to understand these issues. I'll tell you what the law currently is, what changes may occur, and what your strategy should be. I have very specific suggestions about what you can plan now and what changes you may need to make when the law changes. I also think some of the coming changes may be temporary, not permanent. My purpose here is to show you how to understand these areas. Then you'll be able to roll out the right strategies to protect your assets, your business, and your family.

If you don't think you and your family need planning and protection, think again. I've seen people suffer severe financial and personal losses that could easily have been avoided with good planning. The fact that there are changes coming to the tax system should focus your interest on planning. Your new or updated plan should retain, and even enhance, your flexibility.

Personalized Planning is the Only Successful Planning. An essential step towards understanding estate and wealth planning is to personalize the process. As you examine the strategies I present, ask yourself: "How does this apply to me, my family, my business, and my goals?" This is not the part of life where one size fits all. You need to make informed choices and there are quite a few planning strategies and tools to choose from. You need to focus on the result you're trying to accomplish and evaluate your options in light of their ability to help you accomplish your particular goals. Some tools won't fit your family's goals or personal preferences. If that's the case, they're not good ideas for you to adopt.

Before you decide to avoid particular tools or strategies, though, you need to understand them. Sometimes, your initial reaction to an idea may be negative for no apparent reason. If you react negatively, you need to study the strategy to assure yourself that your resistance isn't just fear of the unknown. Once you come to understand a particular strategy, however, don't be afraid to reject it if it doesn't feel right to you. Even if a strategy is mathematically better, if it doesn't fit you and your family's values, plans and situation, it's not right for you.

There are a number of potential tools for minimizing investment and tax risk to your family and business. Please don't be impressed by how interesting or exotic a tool itself is. Nor should you be impressed by anyone just because they're a master of a particular tool. The legal craftsman's task is to select the best tool in light of the job to be done. A perfectly executed Charitable Remainder Annuity Trust, or CRAT (the subject of Chapter 16), may delight your attorney and accountant; however, it may or may not be what you really need.

Your role isn't to memorize the steps to set up these strategies or to pass an exam. It's much more important. You need to use this information to focus your planning. Once you understand the available planning strategies, what these strategies can do, and how they worked, or didn't work for other people, you'll be able to refine and better articulate specific, achievable goals for yourself, your family, and your business.

Wealth Planning. The fundamental concept behind modern investment planning is sometimes called behavioral investing, and the central idea is the role of proper asset allocation.

How individuals invest differs fundamentally from how institutions invest. There's a very ingrained behavioral pattern in most of us that makes it difficult to be a good investor. It's hard not to be emotional about your financial life, and emotionally driven choices may not be good ones. Mathematical perfection alone isn't the key either, because your happiness also depends on how well your plan fits your life and your values.

Individuals tend to invest based on fear-and-greed. Many individuals flock to investments that experienced large gains in the immediate past, in hopes of sharing in the growth they just saw. That's the greed part. Similarly, when a particular part of the market did badly in the recent past, many people shy away from it. That's the fear part.

Institutions don't have as hard a time avoiding fear-and-greed style investing. That doesn't mean institutional investors are always profitable. It only means discipline is easier to come by when professional analysts are investing corporate money. It's easier to be cool if it isn't your family's financial future on the line. The best individual investors can learn from the discipline that the institutions have developed.

Look at different groups or classes of assets in the investment market, and compare their performance over a period of years. You'll be struck by the fact that there's significant change in the performance of different classes of investments, year by year.

Figure 2-1 is organized to show returns from nine different classes of investments.

Asset Classes and Returns

1997	1998	1999	2000	2001	2002	2003
US Large Cap 33%	US Large Cap 29%	Emerging Markets 66%	Mid Cap 18%	Corp Bonds 9.7%	Global Bonds 16%	Emerging Markets 56%
Mid Cap 32%	Internat'l Stocks 20%	Internat'l Stocks 27%	US Gov Bonds 13%	US Gov Bonds 7%	US Gov Bonds 11.5%	Small Cap 47%
Small Cap 22%	Mid Cap 19%	Small Cap 21%	Corp Bonds 9.5%	High Yld Bonds 5%	Corp Bonds 10%	Internat'l Stocks 20%
High Yld Bonds 13%	Global Bonds 13%	US Large Cap 21%	Global Bonds 5%	Global Bonds 3%	High Yld. Bonds -1.5%	Mid Cap 36%
US Gov Bonds 9.6%	US Gov Bonds 9.8%	Mid Cap 15%	Small Cap -3%	Small Cap 2.5%	Emerging Markets -6%	High Yld Bonds 29%
Corp Bonds 8%	Corp Bonds 8%	High Yld Bonds 2%	High Yld Bonds -6%	Mid Cap -.6%	Mid Cap -14%	US Large Cap 27%
Global Bonds 3%	High Yld Bonds 2%	Corp Bonds .2%	US Large Cap -9%	Emerging Markets -2.4%	Internat'l Stocks -16%	Global Bonds 23%
Internat'l Stocks 2%	Small Cap -3%	US Gov Bonds -2%	Internat'l Stocks -13%	US Large Cap -11%	Small Cap -20%	Corp Bonds 7%
Emerging Markets -12%	Emerging Markets -25%	Global Bonds -3.5%	Emerging Markets -31%	Internat'l Stocks -21%	US Large Cap -22%	US Gov Bonds 2%

Figure 2-1

13

Each column represents one year, and each box shows the return from one investment class for that year. Read from left to right, the columns cover the years 1997 to 2003. The boxes are restacked for each year, so the asset class with highest returns is shown at the top of the column, and the asset class with the lowest returns is shown at the bottom. Let's focus on the year 1999. In 1999, U.S. Large Cap stocks, located 4th from the top of the column, had a 21% positive return. In that same year, as shown in Figure 2-2, the U.S. Government bond market, two boxes from the bottom of the column, showed a negative total return of approximately -2%.

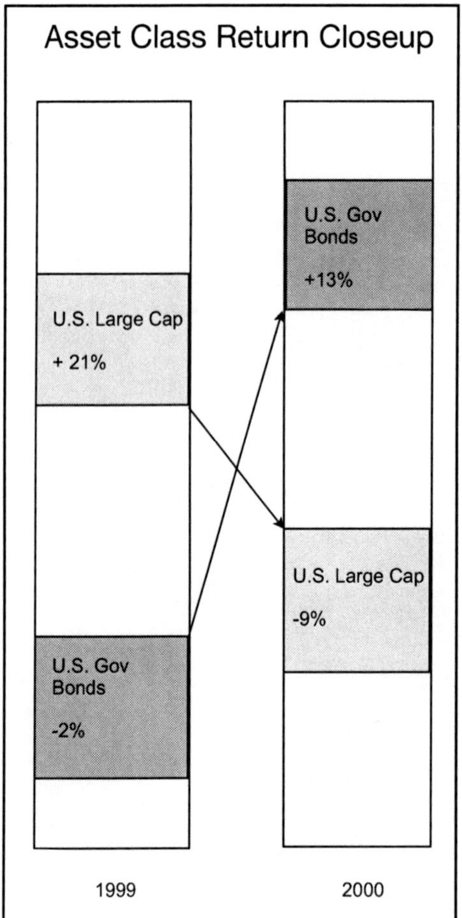

An investor motivated by fear-and-greed would shrink from the negative return from U.S. Government bonds, and at the end of 1999 sell any he had in his portfolio. He'd also be attracted by the positive return in U.S. Large Cap stocks and be buying them heavily at the end of 1999.

Now examine the column for the year 2000. U.S. Large Cap stocks, where our investor just bought heavily, had a large loss with the index showing a negative 9% return for the year. Our investor sold off his U.S. Government bonds at the end of 1999. Sadly for him, U.S. Government bonds had an excellent year in 2000, ending 13% higher.

Asset Class Return Closeup

U.S. Gov Bonds +13%

U.S. Large Cap + 21%

U.S. Large Cap -9%

U.S. Gov Bonds -2%

1999   2000

Figure 2-2

There are many other examples of this phenomenon. Emerging Markets went from the worst performer in 1998 at -25%, to the highest in 1999 with more than 60% return. Emerging Markets then went back to being the worst performer in 2000 with a -31% return, and was back to being the top performer in 2003 at a positive 56% return.

Those who invest purely on the fear-and-greed model are buying things that just rose and selling things that just fell. As a result, they'll generally be behind the curve. Market turnarounds happen fairly quickly, and rarely in a uniform manner. Buying or selling investment assets based on the performance of those assets in the immediate past is a poor way of picking investments. You'd be best off if you could time the markets – that is, if you could pick which areas of the economy are about to go up, or down, in advance. The problem is that timing a market is just about impossible.

Modern Portfolio Theory and Asset Allocation. Why do these concepts matter? They are the underpinnings of a real revolution in modern portfolio theory. It started with analytical work done by Harry Markowitz beginning in the 1950's, leading eventually to a Nobel Prize for him, along with William Sharp and Merton Miller.

The essence of their work is counter-intuitive to the individual investor. Markowitz and his colleagues proved mathematically that most of the gains in a portfolio come from proper allocation of funds among asset classes rather than from picking individual stocks or securities. Specifically, investment theories based upon picking the hot stock don't work. That's not to say investors shouldn't pay any attention to details about the individual securities they invest in, but individual investors should put more emphasis than they normally do on entire asset classes.

Institutions create a balanced portfolio of investments by paying close attention to the proportional mix of various classes of assets in the portfolio. In other words, balancing the asset classes correctly is more attainable, and more important, than trying to pick the hot stock. The individual investor who wishes to adopt this method needs to pick a diversified portfolio of investments from the different asset classes that matches his risk preference, growth plans, and cash flow needs.

The other aspect to the modern portfolio model is the need to periodically rebalance the portfolio. Once investments have been selected, there will be market driven changes in their value over time. When the values change, some parts of the portfolio grow and others shrink. At defined intervals, the mix of asset classes in the portfolio must be re-balanced. This required re-balancing is another aspect of modern portfolio theory that's counter-intuitive for an individual investor.

Suppose our fear-and-greed style individual investor experiences growth in some areas of his portfolio. Assume, for example, that U.S. Large Cap Stocks are doing well this year. Assume that as a class, these stocks have grown about 20% in a year. Unless everything else in the portfolio also grew at 20%, the balance of investment classes in the portfolio is no longer the same. Assume, also, that bonds in the portfolio fell in value this year. Under modern portfolio theory, the portfolio now contains too much of the growing asset class, large cap stocks, and too little of the shrinking one, bonds. The investor needs to reallocate his funds to create the correct proportional mix of asset classes in the portfolio. The investor does this by selling off part of the gain from rising asset classes and investing the funds in a lower growth asset class. In our example, the investor would sell stocks and buy bonds.

In the simplest terms, to rebalance a portfolio correctly the investor must sell off winners and put the money into losers. This is counter-intuitive for investors motivated by fear-and-greed. But putting more money into recent winners and selling off recent losers, based on the fear-and-greed model, is guaranteed to lead to a poorly balanced portfolio.

A well chosen portfolio structure, rebalanced periodically, generates more return for lower risk. An economist would say it has a lower standard deviation and is closer to the individual's efficient investment frontier. Standard deviation refers to volatility; in other words, an asset with lower standard deviation is less volatile. Being closer to the efficient investment frontier refers to getting the most return for a given level of risk. The balanced portfolio makes money more smoothly with less risk for a given level of return.

There's no guaranteed portfolio that's right for everyone; the mix of asset classes depends on your risk preferences, cash flow needs and your level of wealth. It will also change over time as your life changes. However, unlike impossible plans calling for the investor to pick the hot stocks, or to time the market, a balanced portfolio is something that an individual investor can successfully create and maintain.

If your total investable wealth is small, you may need to select mutual funds to diversify across some asset classes. A modest investment in a mutual fund gives the investor the ability to participate in the large variety of stocks the fund holds. The disadvantages to mutual funds are the expenses of management fees and brokerage fees taken from the funds invested, and the fact that tax losses are shared with all fund members. If you have more money to invest, you'll be better off owning a portfolio of securities directly so that the tax and investment strategies are tailored to your needs.

CHAPTER 3:

Avoiding Bad
Planning Strategies

Chapter Contents: Avoiding Planning Danger From the Internet ▶ "Psst – Hey Mister – How About a Cheap Trust?" ▶ Paying for an Older Parent's Trust

"Life is what happens to you while
you're busy making other plans."
John Lennon (1940–1980)

Avoid Planning Danger From the Internet. Some people get a kick out of figuring out answers to questions by using the Internet. If this applies to you, feel free. But remember that many legitimate and helpful websites exist alongside many others with wrong, dangerous or dishonest information. It isn't easy to tell the difference between the good and bad unless you're well informed.

Let's cruise the information superhighway for a moment or two looking for trouble. The sites I'm presenting weren't things I had to look long and hard for; they came up on the first page of my first search using "Estate Planning" as the search parameter on a popular browser.

The first two sites I found said nothing of substance, just "please contact us, we do planning." The third website I found listed on the search results was an all-out disaster. It gives a list of steps that they think everyone should follow, and practically all the advice it gave was bad. The website's information is in quotation marks, slightly rewritten because of the poor grammar on the original page. My comments, in italics, follow each of the website's 5 "must do" points:

1.   "You must write out a will! If you die without a will, your estate ends up in probate court!"

So if you do have a will, you won't have to go through probate? Wrong. Rely on this advice, and you or your family will have a year or more of delay, and tens of thousands of dollars less in assets.

2.   "In addition to your will, you must have a durable power of attorney."

Do you need a durable power of attorney? It depends. There's a health-care durable power of attorney, and whether or not you need one is strictly a matter of personal preference. I discuss this, and the financial power of attorney, which is often used improperly, in Chapter 17. It's wrong to say that powers of attorney are a "must have" item for everyone.

3.   "You'll save money and time by using estate planning software! Prepare your legal documents with a software package, and have your attorney review them. Also, the planning questions in the software will help you organize yourself and save time and money."

Will this save you money? Generally not! If you bring me a document prepared by someone else and ask whether or not it is correct, I'll need to review the entire document. That will take me longer than preparing the documents myself using language I'm already very familiar with. I suppose I do agree with part of the advice on this one though. I agree that questionnaires are good for planning. Mine's available at my website, (www.TheWisePlanner.com) and it will help you organize your information and records.

4.   "Make sure you have your will notarized."

Notarize your will? Why? Notarizing is used to demonstrate the validity of signatures, usually for documents that may be recorded at the county recorder's office. Failure to notarize a will doesn't invalidate it. The rules for witnessing a will aren't uniform from state to state. If you live in California you need the will to be formally witnessed by two witnesses, not one, and if neither is a notary, the will is still valid.

5.   "Review your will frequently. The laws change and you need to be constantly vigilant."

Not really. The law does change from time to time, but it's more likely that changes in your life, rather than changes in the law, will require a change in your plan. This is the type of information you will be aware of long before your lawyer. For example, your lawyer won't know if you've just had another child, had a divorce, or experienced a death in the family, but you will. A major life change means you need to examine your estate plan to see if it needs to be changed as well.

Keep in mind that anyone can create a website with ten dollars for a name registration, a few bucks every month for web hosting, and some time. Some internet sites are created and maintained by people who are experts in their fields, and others by people who are as crazy as two waltzing mice. Your finances are important to you and your family, so be careful.

"Psst – Hey Mister – How About a Cheap Trust?" Should you try to draw up your own estate plan? No. Of course it appears to cost less if you do it yourself. Shouldn't the real bargain hunters among us use self help books, or the no-lawyer-needed discount estate planners you sometimes see in newspaper ads? Please don't. Chances are good that what you will create, or have created, will save you money now but will cost more at the time of your death.

Why? Let me give you an example. Most people drive a car. Most of us know our car is powered by an engine that burns gasoline to turn the wheels. Most folks know that the car has controls used for starting, stopping, and steering in traffic. A few very stubborn individuals refuse, on principal, to understand the car at all. They are at the mercy of the car salesmen and mechanics. A few other people know so much about cars that they can rebuild a transmission. What do you need to understand to use your car? You need to know enough about the car to operate it safely, but you don't need to become an automobile mechanic.

Estate planning, wealth management and asset protection planning work just the same way. Knowledge is power. It's crucial for you to have this knowledge to protect your wealth and your family's future. You need comprehensive wealth preservation, asset protection and estate planning that is very safe and will work correctly over a long period of time.

What about the guy in the newspaper who advertises a trust for $399? Isn't going to one of these places better than going to a lawyer? Or at least better than not doing anything?

Using a simplified, one-size-fits-all product does work some of the time. Some of the time it doesn't. When it doesn't, your financial security is seriously at risk. Even a recent version of the AARP website had two articles warning about these services:

> "Beware of scams! Beware of "free lunch" estate-planning seminars and other scams that suggest that AARP endorses living trusts. AARP doesn't sell or endorse any living trust product. And trusts sold through these schemes often are more costly and don't comply with state law." *http://www.aarp.org/ money/estate_planning/articles/choice_of_a_lifetime.html*

> "Pre-printed, generic forms are often passed off as custom-made documents. There is often no attorney involved. The package may be overly expensive. The forms may not meet the requirements of state law. And they often don't include clear instructions on how to fund the trust. Poorly drawn or unfunded trusts can cost you money and endanger your best intentions.... Remember: If you want to know if a living trust is right for you, get advice from an estate planning attorney." *http://www.aarp. org/money/estate_planning/articles/truth_about_living_trusts. html*

Your happiness and security are important, so think hard about what you're trying to do. You are trying to protect your business, your home, and your assets. You want to make sure your family is secure, both while you're here, and after you die.

No scare tactics intended, but aren't these the assets you've spent most of your life working for? Are you going to try saving a few hundred, or even a few thousand dollars, and risk doing it wrong, with results that could cause a complete financial meltdown for your family?

The danger with the do-it-yourself kit, or the estate planning service in the newspaper, is that no one will spend time with you to find out what you actually need. No one will educate you as to why you need it. In fact, some cut-rate planning services don't even keep informed as to the changes in the law. Recently, I reviewed a trust put together by an estate planning service that referred to statutes that were repealed in 1992 – the trust was given to the client and signed in 2000. The mistakes in the documents weren't fatal, but it does mean those cut-rate clowns hadn't updated their forms in more than 8 years.

Lawyers often make money off people's misfortune. Sometimes, we make much more than if these people had done appropriate planning. Most lawyers I know, myself included, have handled probate problems where it took tens of thousands of dollars to undo a costly mistake made by the clients. I'd rather spend my time giving good advice and helping people implement good plans. It creates a real sense of satisfaction to do the planning correctly, and I'd rather you do it right the first time.

Here's some more straight talk. Is your total estate, that is the gross value of everything you'll own when you die, very small? If so, you should consider using the statutory will, or writing out your own will. I'll give more details in Chapter 6. This only makes sense if your estate is small enough, and if there's nothing complicated about your wishes for the disposition of your property. If your finances are tight and your assets very small, and if you're smart, patient, and careful, this is probably your best bet. Just be careful, and if you have more than a very small estate, remember you're better off investing in some good planning.

Paying for an Older Parent's Trust. When an older person is on a very restricted budget, adult children sometimes offer to pay for the estate planning process. These adult children realize that the tax and probate savings will recoup much more than the cost of the plan.

This is a farsighted use of funds and wholly appropriate in most cases. The only drawback is the possibility of a conflict of interest. Whenever an attorney is paid by one person, but does work for the benefit of another, there's the theoretical possibility of a conflict of interest. In estate planning, generally there's no actual conflict because both the person making the plan and the person paying the bill want the same result, to save taxes and probate fees. However, the two parties sometimes want different things. For example, an older parent may want the assets to be distributed differently than the younger family member offering to pay for the plan, so an actual conflict of interests can arise in such a case.

The attorney must uphold the interest of the person the attorney is creating the plan for, not the one who is paying the bill. If there's a real divergence in the interests of the beneficiaries and the trustors, an ethical attorney may find himself unable to effectively represent either person. In such a case the attorney would have to quit. However, this seldom happens. In the majority of cases the trustors and beneficiaries have similar goals, and it is perfectly appropriate for one person to pay the legal fees associated with another person's estate plan.

CHAPTER 4:

Where We're Going With Tax Laws

Chapter Contents: The 50,000 Foot View: Understanding EGTRRA and Beyond ▶ The Previous System ▶ The Gift Tax and the Estate Tax ▶ The Present System ▶ The Future System ▶ Key Areas For Change

"The hardest thing in the world to understand is income tax."
Attributed to Albert Einstein (1879–1955)

This Chapter addresses the tax law governing asset transfers, specifically the estate tax, gift tax and capital gains taxes. First, I'll explain how the system worked in the past, then the current (2009/10) system, and finally what's likely for the future. Currently I'm giving you an overview from the 50,000 foot level, but I've included much more detail about these subjects in later chapters.

The 50,000 Foot View: Understanding EGTRRA and Beyond. At your death, your material possessions will pass to others and this will have important tax consequences. The Economic Growth and Tax Relief Reconciliation Act of 2001, or EGTRRA, set huge changes in motion for estate and gift tax. The rates of tax, the exemptions, and linkages between estate and gift tax, and the effects of capital gains tax are issues already affected by these changes, and all of these will change again.

The Previous System. Prior to EGTRRA, estate tax and gift tax were linked. The tax rates and exemptions to the tax had also been relatively stable for many years. Speaking in general terms, the estate and gift tax system worked as follows: Each taxpayer was granted a single exemption from tax in the amount of $600,000, adjusted annually for inflation. Lifetime gifts and post-death bequests were subject to gift or estate tax, respectively, once the $600,000 exemption was exceeded. The tax rate was steep, rapidly reaching a maximum rate above 50%. By the way, the linkage between estate and gift taxes is easily explained, and in case it isn't clear, let me go through it in more detail.

The Gift Tax and the Estate Tax. The American estate tax system is now a true estate tax. The law examines a decedent's assets, calls it an estate, and calculates and collects tax from those assets. Quite a few years ago, America had an inheritance tax system, and many other countries have this system today. Under inheritance tax systems, the tax is collected from the person getting the inheritance.

Why is there a gift tax as well as an estate tax? Picture wealthy dad, on his deathbed, saying "Kids, (gasp, cough), if you get my money only after I die, there's a big estate tax on it. Here, (cough, gasp), I'll give it to you while I'm still alive. This way there's no estate tax on it (wheeze)." If dad can time this transfer to his last few minutes on earth, the amount transferred would not be subject to estate tax. Congress prevented this hypothetical trick long ago, by establishing the gift tax. Gift tax is calculated from the same tables and with the same exclusions as the estate tax and is applied to transfers made while the taxpayer is alive. Now, our little deathbed scene has an extra bit at the end, where one of the kids says, "Forget it, Pop, they tax gifts, too."

This linkage between estate and gift taxes was designed to avoid double dipping by taxpayers who make both pre-death and post-death gifts. It uses a single exemption amount that's applied to both estate tax and gift tax. The first $600,000 transfered, whether during life or after death, was the exempt amount and is tax free. All amounts over that are taxable. If wealthy dad gave his kids $1,000,000 during his lifetime, then the first $600,000 of that transfer used up his tax exemption, and he paid gift tax on $400,000 the year he made the gift. When wealthy dad later dies, if he has another $1,000,000 in his estate, the entire amount is taxable; the exemption was used up by gifting while he was alive.

In theory, you need to track every gift a person makes in his lifetime for this system to work. Otherwise you don't know how much of the exemption amount, if any, is left when that person dies. A gift tax system does, in fact, exist, and significant gifts should be reported in the year they are made on a gift tax return. This is true even if the donor's lifetime gifts are still below the exemption amount and there's no tax due. Filing the returns with the IRS permits them to track a taxpayer's exemption amounts, so they can verify what amounts have been used up by lifetime giving and how much exemption remains available at death.

As a practical matter, no one wants to fill out a tax return for every $50 birthday gift they ever made. Since the IRS has never been staffed to cope with that many returns, the law has a minimum built into it. No gift tax return needs to be filed if gifts from a taxpayer to any single recipient, in any given year, are less than $10,000. This amount has been adjusted for inflation, too, and it now stands at $13,000, and it re-sets automatically each year. To summarize, as long as the total a taxpayer gives to any single recipient stays below $13,000 in a single year, it doesn't get counted against gift tax or estate tax exemptions.

Now, back to the general workings of the estate tax. Assume a person who died, or a decedent, had a total estate, or all that he or she owned at death, worth $500,000, see Figure 4-1. Assume that the decedent had made no significant lifetime gifts and died years ago, before 1990. In such a case, no estate taxes were due because the estate is less than the tax exemption amount of $600,000.

Example of Estate Tax Flow and Exemption Usage

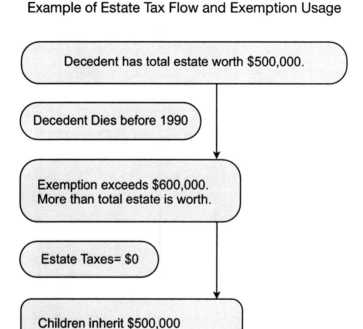

Decedent has total estate worth $500,000.

Decedent Dies before 1990

Exemption exceeds $600,000.
More than total estate is worth.

Estate Taxes= $0

Children inherit $500,000

Figure 4-1

For a second example, Figure 4-2, assume the decedent left a $2,100,000 estate, with no lifetime gifts. Again, the first $600,000 is exempt. The remaining $1,500,000 gets taxed at a rate which starts lower, but quickly hits the maximum rate. For a $2,100,000 estate, the estate tax bill would have been roughly $525,000. Payment of the estate taxes would have been due 9 months after the date of death.

This explains the careful attention taxpayers should pay to this area of the law. It meant that after a certain level of wealth was passed, the taxing authorities were taking half of every additional dollar in an estate, and anywhere from one-quarter to one-half of the total estate was lost to taxes.

Example of Estate Tax Flow and Exemption Usage

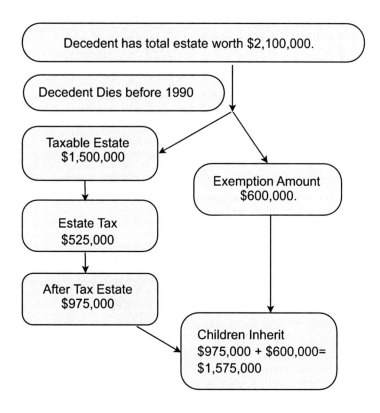

Figure 4-2

The Present System. Starting in 2001, EGTRRA made major changes to the system. These were made according to a schedule, which called for changes to be phased in over a ten year period. The most important changes were to increase the exemption amounts, and slightly decrease the maximum rate for the estate tax. Exemptions went to $1,000,000 in 2002 and 2003, increased to $1,500,000 for deaths in 2004 and 2005, then to $2,000,000 through the end of 2008, and in 2009 the exemptions increased to $3,500,000. The maximum rate at which an estate is taxed gradually decreased from 50% in 2002 to 45% in 2007 where it has remained. In the year 2010, there was scheduled to be an unlimited exemption. An unlimited exemption means that there's no estate tax on the assets of a person dying in that year, regardless of the value of the estate. In the year 2011, we were scheduled to automatically return to a $1,000,000 exclusion and a maximum tax rate of over 50%. This would have returned us to the same exclusion amount and rate that would have existed in 2011 had EGTRRA never been passed.

In addition, under EGTRRA there were two other major changes. The gift tax is no longer linked to the estate tax. Instead, the gift tax exemption has remained constant while the estate tax exemptions changed. The exemption for gift taxes has never increased beyond $1,000,000 and is not scheduled to do so. Also, the capital gains tax may undergo a significant change in 2010. This will take the form of an alteration in the method used to determine the basis of all capital assets transferred at death (more about this in Chapter 12). These are very significant changes, and have generated much uncertainty for anyone who might be affected.

The Future System. In the early part of this decade most tax professionals thought that Congress would act, probably before 2010, to make the phaseout of the estate tax permanent. However, with the shifting landscape of federal law and the increase in the federal deficit, the phase-out of estate tax is not going to happen in the short term, and the long term results are far from certain.

Over the last ten years, there has been tremendous discord in Congress about how to fix the estate tax system. For example, from 2004 to 2007 the House passed three bills to permanently repeal the estate tax, and two bills to modify but retain the tax, while the Senate did not pass any legislation during those three years addressing estate tax. In the 2008-2009 session of Congress, seven bills to permanently repeal the estate tax were introduced in the House and four in the Senate. Seven bills to retain but modify the estate tax were introduced in the House and one was introduced in the Senate. There were significant differences between the various bills, and Congress has reached no consensus on the proposed changes, although President Obama has announced that he will continue the 2009 tax levels forward into the future. Please check my website, *www.TheWisePlanner.com*, to see the latest developments.

Key Areas for Change. The areas that you should be most attentive to for changes in the immediate future are the estate tax rates and the basic exemption amounts. In addition, there will be changes that relate to other taxes, particularly gift taxes, generation skipping taxes, and the income/capital gains tax, but these changes will probably be dependent on the estate tax rate and exemption changes.

It has taken so long to resolve the outstanding uncertainty, and consensus is so lacking, that despite the President's announcement, the first change enacted by Congress, to extend the tax rate from 2009, may be only temporary. I discuss this in detail in Chapter 12.

CHAPTER 5:

The Ins and Outs of Wealth Transfer, Part 1

Chapter Contents: What Happens to You After You Pass Away ▸ Why Some People Don't Plan Well ▸ How Our Society Tracks and Transfers Legal Ownership ▸ Dying Without A Plan ▸ The High Cost of Dying ▸ Welcome to Probate Court ▸ The Probate Process ▸ Non-Probate Assets

"CHAPTER XXIV. HOW THE GREAT KAAN CAUSETH THE BARK OF TREES, MADE INTO SOMETHING LIKE PAPER, TO PASS FOR MONEY OVER ALL HIS COUNTRY....He makes them take of the bark of a certain tree.... and this they make into something resembling sheets of paper.... All these pieces of paper are issued with as much solemnity and authority as if they were of pure gold or silver;.... And the Kaan causes every year to be made such a vast quantity of this money, which costs him nothing, that it must equal in amount all the treasure in the world...."

The Travels of Marco Polo, Marco Polo
(1254–1326)

This Chapter will explain how money and other assets are passed from one generation to another. In fact, there are quite a few different methods, and some are far safer and more efficient than others.

What Happens to You After You Pass Away. That's an interesting metaphysical question, but that answer is in a different book. The question I can help you answer is what happens to your material possessions when you die. I can also advise you on how to take the most effective steps you can to ensure that your possessions are protected and your wishes for their distribution are carried out.

Material possessions are important to us. If you watch the victim of a fire, flood, or earthquake, you'll see that they always fight hard to preserve what they can and grieve over what they lose. It's human nature. If you are a business owner, you have spent years building up your business. You've been investing in infrastructure and paying taxes, creating and then executing your business plan. Your family's assets, your home and your investments need to stay safe. Whether large or small, years of earnings and savings went into them. For many folks, these assets represent more than one generation's earnings and savings.

Take a few minutes to think about the personal freedom and security that your assets represent and what you'd lose if they were gone. Think about the things you'd like for your family and how you need to be careful and do your best to provide for them.

Now, imagine that there's an evil genius, out of a Hollywood action movie, and he wants your assets. He can freeze your bank account and drain it if you don't cooperate. He can even force the sale of your home. He will work slowly, unwinding his evil plan over many years, and before you've escaped his clutches, a ransom of hundreds of thousands, or even millions of dollars must be paid. As much as half of all the wealth that you accumulated during your life must be surrendered before your children or grandchildren can touch any of the money.

This is a fantasy. There's no criminal genius doing all these things. Of course, that's the only part that's a fantasy. There are political and legal systems at work right now that will do all that I've described unless you successfully plan around them.

I'm not against paying taxes. We all need, and use, many things provided by tax dollars. Police and fire protection, libraries, and roads are public benefits that need to be paid for. However, using legitimate structures and strategies as tools to minimize the tax burden for yourself and your family is something you can and should plan to do.

If you understand the framework of the legal and social issues that are behind the asset management and wealth transfer process, you'll be able to make an effective plan that will work for you. On my website, *www.TheWisePlanner.com*, I include a checklist of information you need to gather for an effective wealth preservation and estate planning session, and a simple framework for evaluating your income and expenses. Although gathering the information is important, the first step is understanding what you're trying to accomplish. Then you'll know what steps you'll have to take to help you hold and transition your wealth securely.

Why Some People Don't Plan Well. Some people don't plan because they don't see the benefits. Some don't plan because they are lazy. Others don't plan because they're stubborn. One client came up with a very original reason he wanted a simple will and nothing more. He owned a house worth around $600,000. I explained to him that he would likely spend a year to a year and a half in probate court and spend thousands of dollars in fees if all he used for his estate plan was a simple will. He corrected me, saying: "I won't be spending any money, or experiencing any delay. I'll be dead."

That's true, but his family will have to deal with the time delay and money problems. He didn't seem to care about the delay or the expense to them; he just wanted to spend as little money as possible while he was alive. I drafted his simple will and his estate plan, according to his wishes, in just about the cheapest way possible. When he passes away, though, his heirs will likely be very irritated, because they will have to do all the hard work involved in probate instead of using the smoother transition provided by a trust.

How Our Society Tracks and Transfers Legal Ownership. Ownership of material possessions is complicated, both while you're alive and after you die. There are several different legal and social systems that come into play, and they aren't well synchronized with each other. But they do have an important impact on your property during your life and after you die.

Proving that we own specific things is important. I'm looking at a framed photograph as I write this. It's a vacation shot of myself, my wife and our children. I don't have an ownership certificate for it. I received an invoice or receipt when I purchased the camera, and another when I bought the picture frame, but I didn't keep them. It's not because I'm careless (believe me, I'm not). Nobody can, or should, keep invoices for everything they ever bought. It would be completely impractical. I have no proof that I own the picture other than my word and the fact that it hangs on my office wall.

We live under legal and regulatory systems which recognize that some personal property requires no ownership documentation. For such property, nothing but possession is required to establish ownership.

Bearer bonds, used as a plot device in many movies, are a good example. They can be cashed or used by whoever holds them. These assets aren't much of a problem to transfer when the owner dies as long as the heirs get physical access to them.

However, most significant financial assets are tracked by legal and regulatory systems which identify the owner's name and the asset involved. Cars are registered at the Department of Motor Vehicles. Deeds for real estate are recorded at the office of the County Recorder. Financial institutions, banks, and brokerage houses track ownership of assets by using the name of the account holder as stated in the paperwork when the account is opened. For smaller companies, like privately owned corporations, the company's share register and the paper share certificates themselves are issued with the owner's name on them to acknowledge and track ownership of shares in the company.

Why is this important? While you're alive, proof of ownership only matters when you buy, sell or borrow. And if there's some sort of problem, you're there to handle it. However, the legal and financial systems regulating proof of ownership do not cope well with assets owned by someone who has passed away. Any transfers, or other changes in ownership, need to be made within the rules regulating those systems. Without planning, your most valuable and useful assets cannot be used by your family or heirs after you pass away. Before they can buy, sell, borrow against, or otherwise use your assets, your family or heirs must comply with some difficult and expensive requirements imposed by these legal and financial systems.

Dying Without a Plan. If you die without a will, you have died intestate, which is law Latin for "without a will." Without a plan, your estate will be probated and distributed to your heirs under the laws of intestate succession. The intestate succession laws determine who gets the assets of the decedent without any concern or regard for your personal preferences. These laws distribute assets strictly according to a statutory list embedded in the probate code, the so-called tables of consanguinity. Under the rules set out by these laws, your assets could pass much differently than you may have wished. If you wish to leave unequal shares to heirs, or wish to assure that someone you're related to does not get part of your estate, don't die without a plan.

According to the legal order established by the tables of consanguinity in California, if you're unmarried and die intestate, your property passes to your children. If you're unmarried and have no children, your property passes to your parents. If they're no longer living, your property passes to your brothers and sisters, then to grandparents, then to more remote kin. This is all done according to a statutory family tree contained in the table of consanguinity. If none of the heirs can be found, the estate will escheat, and be distributed to the state in which you reside.

If you're married when you die intestate, property is treated differently according to its legal status as community or separate property. This can get tricky, because an asset can be partly community property and partly separate property at the same time. All community property goes to the surviving spouse of the person who dies intestate. For separate property, if the decedent left no will and had a spouse but no children or other relatives, the spouse gets all of the separate property in addition to the community property. With a spouse and one child, one-half of the separate property will pass to the surviving spouse and one-half to the child. If the decedent leaves a surviving spouse and two or more children, then one-third of the separate property will pass to the surviving spouse and two-thirds will pass to the children.

There are other unfortunate aspects to dying without a plan in place. If you pass away leaving a child under the age of 18 with no other surviving parent, a guardian is needed for that child. In the absence of any effective plan, this guardian will be chosen by a court. The guardian will report annually to the court until the child reaches age 18. The court will also appoint an administrator to handle your estate during the probate proceedings, usually the first person who files a petition. This may not be the person you would have selected.

The High Cost of Dying. The probate process is expensive, and here is an example using California law. The Probate Code provides for statutory fees to be paid to the personal representative, that is, the executor or administrator, of the decedent's estate. The same amount of money is paid to the attorney for the personal representative. Statutory fees are based on the gross fair market value of the estate. The fee, at the time I write this, is four percent (4%) of the first $100,000.00; three percent (3%) of the next $100,000.00; two percent (2%) of the next $800,000.00; one percent (1%) of the next $9,000,000, one half of one per cent (1/2%) of the next $15,000,000. If the estate is larger than $25,000,000, the fee is not specified in the statute but will be decided on by the Probate Court.

Example: Probate estate of $2,000,000 (Gross Value)

four percent (4%) of $100,000=	$ 4,000
three percent (3%)of $100,000=	$ 3,000
two percent (2%) of $800,000=	$ 16,000
one percent (1%) of $1,000,000=	$ 10,000
TOTAL	$ 33,000

The total commission to the executor, for an estate of $2,000,000 would be $33,000. The attorney would receive an equal amount, so the estate must pay a total of $66,000. You should be aware that the computation is based on the gross value of the estate, not the net value. For example, if you own a home with a gross value of $1.2 million, that $1.2 million is part of the value of your estate for fee calculations. The fee calculation ignores any debt against the property. If you owe the bank $800,000 on the mortgage when you die, the net value of the asset is only $400,000, but your estate is still charged a fee as though the home is worth $1.2 million.

The attorney and executor may also charge extra fees to the estate for extraordinary services such as overseeing the sale of property. There is also a court filing fee, based on the size of the estate and ranging from hundreds to thousands of dollars, for the filing of the petition to initiate probate. There is a fee to be paid to the probate referee based on the size of those assets of the estate that need appraising (and the law requires appraisal of everything but cash). The referee fee is roughly 0.1% of the total value of those assets. There may also be fees for accounting services, as well as for real estate brokerage commissions or stock brokerage fees if any assets need to be sold to raise cash for the estate.

Why is this so complicated, expensive, and time consuming? Questions of who gets what, or whether a will is authentic were part of the historic origin of the probate system. Modern probate, except in rare cases, isn't primarily about these issues. If probate was just about seeing that assets are distributed to the proper beneficiaries, all you would need to do when someone dies is determine whether there's a will. If not, then examine the statutory rules for intestacy to determine who gets what. If there is a will, make sure the copy filed with the court is authentic and legally sufficient. Then examine it to determine who gets what. If that were all there was to it, most probate cases could be handled in half an hour to half a day!

But the average probate case, in California, takes a year to a year and a half. Why? A short example will take us to the real crux of this important problem. Pretend you work as a bank teller, and you're helping a customer with a question:

Customer: "My Uncle Ray just passed away. There's a little less than five thousand dollars in his checking account. Can I have the money?"

Your response: "No. Sorry."

Customer: "But I'm his closest family member. Heck, I brought a list of all of Uncle Ray's other relatives, and they're all dead. I'm the only living relative he had, and he wanted me to have the money."

Your response: "In the interest of being helpful, I can give you the money if you can bring Uncle Ray in to approve it. Or if Uncle Ray can't come in, get him to sign a release form, saying it's OK to give the money to you."

Customer: "What's wrong with you? Uncle Ray can't come in or sign anything. I told you, he's dead. I've got his death certificate right here."

Your response: "Being dead is no excuse. We can't give his money to you without his permission. Tomorrow, if a different relative shows up looking for the same money, and we gave it to you today, we'd have a problem. If you can't get Uncle Ray to release the money, then you need a court order that says it's safe for us to give you the money."

Customer: "How long will it take to get this court order, and what will it cost? Is it difficult?"

Your response: "You'll have to ask the probate court about that."

Welcome to Probate Court. The reason that probate continues to exist in the modern world is that dead people can't sign their names. Without permission from the dead owner, legal and financial custodians don't want to distribute assets. They take the chance of being wrong when they make these distributions, and bankers hardly ever hold séances. To avoid the risk of litigation over distribution of the property of a dead person, the banker requires the living heirs to go to court and obtain permission for the banker to put the assets into the hands of the living beneficiaries.

Is going to probate a good thing? No, never. Well, hardly ever. If there are significant potential problems with claims by creditors and contingent liabilities in an estate, probate provides a way of clearing up these liabilities. For example, if an architect, lawyer, or broker passes away, and other parties have claims against him, his attorney can file a petition in the probate court and probate all or part of the decedent's estate. Since one of the steps in probate is to invoke the court's claims procedures, this gives other parties notice, and an opportunity to make any claims they have against the decedent. Through the probate process, each claim can be disputed or settled in an organized and controlled environment, namely, the courts.

This type of strategy isn't used frequently. With rare exceptions, probate burns large amounts of time and money and should be avoided. It will cost tens of thousands of dollars or even more and waste months or years of time! But if you don't have an effective plan to prevent it, your estate is almost certainly going to go through probate.

The Probate Process. What, exactly, is probate? Hmmm... let's start with an easier question. What, exactly, is football? In a casual conversation, the usual answer is: "It's a game." That's the simplest answer. It started as a game, but it's become much more. In reality, football is a complex and huge economic engine. It drives substantial income for the participants, owners and organizers by providing entertainment.

'What is Probate?' is also a subtle and complex question. Probate is a court proceeding. A document, generally called a petition, is prepared and filed with the court. Filing the petition initiates a probate case. Filing means the petition is physically taken to the courthouse, a fee paid, and a numbered file is created by the court. The petition is stamped with the case number, date, and time, and is placed in the file. In certain systems this is done with electronic documents rather than paper ones, but the effect is the same.

After the initial filing, there are certain events or tasks which must be done in all probate cases and some that only happen in certain circumstances. There are fees associated with the filing, and fees associated with valuation of the assets by a court-appointed expert, called the Probate Referee. There are fees associated with the attorney's work and fees for the work of the administrator or executor. There are fees if real estate, stocks, or other assets must be sold or purchased during the course of the proceedings. There may be more fees to accountants or additional attorneys' fees for interim or final reporting to the court.

Did you detect a theme developing here? The word 'fee' is used seven times in the preceding paragraph. Probate is expensive, sometimes crushingly so. It's also time consuming. Average probate cases take a year to a year and a half to resolve; complex probate cases may take many years. And, like other civil cases, documents in a probate case file are a matter of public record. This means that anyone can examine the probate file at the courthouse, and learn all of the information related to that estate. In a typical probate case, the identity and value of every important piece of property will be part of the court's file and open to the public.

At the end of a probate case, the court creates formal, binding court orders. These orders give permission to bankers, title companies, and other legal and financial institutions to honor the instructions of the decedent and to change the name of the owner of an asset from the name of the decedent to the name of a living heir. With such a court order in hand, the keepers of these legal and financial systems can make the changes without fear of being challenged. So the answer to the question, "Will my heirs have to go through Probate?" is yes, unless you successfully plan your way around it. Otherwise, without the court order, your family will never be able to use your assets.

Non-Probate Assets. There are some assets that should never have to go through probate. When you first opened an IRA, for example, or bought an insurance policy, you filled out paperwork designating the beneficiaries to receive these items when you die. In the case of assets like IRAs, retirement accounts, or insurance policies, the beneficiary designation will cause the assets to pass to those you designated with no further action from you or your successor trustee. These non-probate assets never need a probate court order; the custodians in charge of these systems of wealth management already have your instructions from your beneficiary designation. Upon your death, they have the power to deliver the assets as you directed, without court order or other delay. Remember, though, if you adopt a child, get divorced, or your life changes in other significant ways you need to update these designations.

CHAPTER 6:

The Ins and Outs
of Wealth Transfer,
Part 2

Chapter Contents: Avoiding Probate ▶ The Complete Basic Menu ▶ Option 1: Do Nothing ▶ Option 2: Using Ownership, or How You Hold Title to Property, as Your Estate Plan ▶ Option 3: How About A Simple Will? ▶ Option 4: What About a Will With a Testamentary Trust?

"My dad told me how to make a small fortune gambling.
First, you start with a large fortune. ..."
Howard Lederer, Poker champion.

Avoiding Probate. Without a plan, your estate will be in probate, with a court appointed administrator, and you'll have lost control over how and when your assets will be distributed. Avoiding probate should now seem like a good idea. But how do you do it?

The Complete Basic Menu. Here are all the possible choices you could make about planning your estate. Some I recommend highly, others I don't. But don't stop reading here. I'll return to each of these items in greater detail later:

1.　　*Do Nothing.* Everyone starts here, but this is not a good place to end. With no plan, you are fully subject to probate fees and delays. Your estate tax liability will be at the maximum level, and you will have no control over where your assets go.

2.　　*Using Ownership, or How You Hold Title to Property, as Your Estate Plan.* Setting up and holding your property as joint tenants with right of survivorship means that the last owner to die gets the asset. This avoids probate, but it's an unstable way to leave your estate. Married couples in community property states can hold property as husband and wife, as community property with right of survivorship. It will pass property efficiently from one spouse to another, but is unstable and may create higher tax liability before the assets pass to your children or other heirs.

3.　　*Creating a Simple Will.* This is what many people have, and it's only slightly better than doing nothing. A will controls which heirs get various possessions, who will be the guardian for minor children, and who will administer the estate. However, with a will, your estate is still subject to maximum probate fees, delays and maximum estate taxes.

4.　　*Creating a Will containing a Testamentary Trust.* This was popular before the 1970's. The trust, created by your will, controls distribution to your heirs over time. The estate may also get estate tax benefits, but your family must still undergo the delay and expense of probate.

5.　　*Creating a Revocable or Living Trust.* For most people, this is the most important component of their estate plan. It avoids probate completely and results in substantial estate tax savings.

6.   *Using Specific Advanced Planning Tools for Particular Needs.* When appropriate, these include strategies such as Insurance Trusts, QPRTs, FLPs, Charitable Remainder Trusts, Special Needs Trusts, and others. These are all described in subsequent chapters.

Looking at this list of possibilities should raise questions in your mind. The most common questions are:

- Why do I need to have an estate plan?
  Without one, you have no control over how your assets are disposed of after your death.

- Where will my assets go without proper planning?
  Because you have no control, assets won't necessarily go where you'd prefer.

- Will my estate need to go through probate?
  Without a plan that avoids it, the probate court will take control of your estate.

- Will there be expenses and fees?
  Probate fees and expenses can cost your estate tens or even hundreds of thousands of dollars.

- Will the process take much time?
  Probates can take years to pass through the court system; while those years pass, your family has very limited control over or access to their assets.

- Will there be higher estate taxes?
  Failure to plan means you don't limit your tax burden. You could pay twice as much in taxes!

Option 1: Do Nothing. The first option is to do nothing. If your situation matches these four factors, doing no planning at all is the best plan:

1. Your assets are, and will always be, too small to be taxable.

2. Intestate succession exactly matches your personal preferences.

3. You don't care if your loved ones experience great expense and lengthy delay before they can use anything that once belonged to you.

4. You're going to live forever.

Doing nothing isn't the best plan for most people.

Option 2: Using Ownership, or How You Hold Title to Property, as Your Estate Plan. When several people acquire real property jointly, they typically take title and hold it as tenants in common. In fact, the law presumes that if people hold property jointly and don't specify their choice, it is held as tenants in common. Tenancy in common is a kind of default provision because it fits the legal and practical expectations most people have about their rights as a co-owner of property. As a tenant in common, sometimes referred to as a TIC, each owner can dispose of his or her fractional portion of the property by gift, sale, or inheritance.

In contrast, holding title to property as joint tenants involves holding property with your co-owners subject to a right of survivorship. By definition, the right of survivorship passes 100% of the property to the surviving co-owner when the other co-owners die. When used as an estate planning device joint tenancy automatically transfers property without the need for probate. The only legal step required is the preparation and recording of a new deed or notice stating that the other joint tenant died and the property now belongs to the survivor(s).

Since it's impossible to be certain that the joint tenancy will continue over time, joint tenancy is not a practical method for estate planning. The owners of joint tenancy property cannot leave their share to another person by will or trust. But if one of the co-owners sells or gives away his portion of the joint tenancy property during his or her lifetime, the joint tenancy is destroyed and the new co-owner becomes a tenant in common with the other owner(s). If this happens, then the property must be disposed of through probate or a trust. This instability makes joint tenancy a poor tool for estate planning.

If a married couple, living in a community property state, inserts the words "community property with right of survivorship" into their deed, they invoke rules that are similar to the joint tenancy rules. This insertion creates the same right of survivorship as joint tenancy, and avoids probate upon the death of one of the spouses. As an added benefit, at the death of the first spouse, the community property receives a step-up in basis to market value for the entire property.

The basis is the original cost to acquire the property, adjusted upwards for any additional costs put into the property for renovations or additions, and lowered for depreciation taken over time on your tax returns. The capital gains tax, from the sale of certain assets, is calculated on the difference between the sale price and the basis. In general, inherited property gets stepped up in basis, so that the inherited portion's basis is adjusted to the market value at the decedent's date of death. In the case of joint tenancy property, the decedent's share of the property gets a step-up in basis to the value as of the date that owner died, but the survivor's share does not. In other words, if the surviving owner sells the property the day his co-owner dies, he pays tax on the gain on his original portion of the investment but there is no capital gains tax on the inherited portion.

Property held as community property with right of survivorship gets a greater benefit. Not just the decedent's half, but all of the community property is stepped-up in basis at the first spouse's death. Please be aware that family issues may weigh against holding assets as community property, and the instability problems that apply to joint tenancy also apply here. Of course, not all states recognize community property as a legal form of ownership. At the time this is written, Arizona, California, Idaho, Louisiana, Nevada, New Mexico, Texas, Washington and Wisconsin are community property states, but be sure to consult with your attorney about the best way for you to hold property.

In certain states, family law and estate planning law give a tax advantage to property that's held as community property. At the death of a spouse, the basis of community property gets stepped up to the market value as of the date of the death. However, separate property retains its original cost basis if the non-owner spouse dies, and when sold, all of the gain is subject to capital gains tax. For estate planning purposes, then, a person might want to change separate property to community property.

If a couple divorces or separates, however, community property should get divided between them while separate property stays with the individual ex-spouse who owns it. For divorce proceedings, a person would rather have separate property rather than community property. Whether your property should be considered community property or separate property can be a complex question, and transmutation of property should not be attempted without the help of a competent lawyer. For more information, see my website at *www.TheWisePlanner. com.*

Option 3: How About A Simple Will? For many years, the simple will was the document most people used for estate planning. In fact, there is a pre-printed form authorized by law in many states. In California, the Probate Code authorizes such a will. The following selected parts of the statutory directions, in Probate Code Section 6240, give succinct information on what a simple form will can, and cannot, do :

"3. Does a Will avoid probate? No. With or without a Will, assets in your name alone usually go through the court probate process....

6. Are there different kinds of Wills? Yes. There are handwritten Wills, typewritten Wills, attorney-prepared Wills, and statutory Wills. All are valid if done precisely as the law requires....

8. Are there any reasons why I should NOT use this Statutory Will? Yes. This is a simple Will. It is not designed to reduce death taxes or other taxes. Talk to a lawyer to do tax planning, especially if (i) your assets will be worth more than $600,000 or the current amount excluded from estate tax under federal law at your death, (ii) you own business-related assets, (iii) you want to create a trust fund for your children's education or other purposes, (iv) you own assets in some other state, (v) you want to disinherit your spouse, domestic partner, or descendants, or (vi) you have valuable interests in pension or profit-sharing plans....

20. What is a trust? There are many kinds of trusts, including trusts created by Wills.... Trusts are too complicated to be used in this Statutory Will. You should see a lawyer if you want to create a trust..."

If your estate isn't small, don't get a simple will. Get professional help and have a Living Trust or other appropriate plan put in place. I don't agree with the statutory instructions that state a will is sufficient if your estate is "less than $600,000 or the exemption amount." I think you shouldn't consider an estate small unless it's much smaller than the exemption amount. Regardless of the exemption amount, there are substantial probate fees and delays you will experience for estates over $100,000.

I've already stated the reason that good planning is important, but it bears repetition. We're considering the final disposition of all of your important assets. For most people, having a well crafted plan in place to pass on your assets safely is critical to peace of mind. If you do it yourself, any mistake you make, or issue you don't consider, won't become clear until you're no longer around, and then it will be too late for you to fix whatever's gone wrong.

Option 4: What About a Will With a Testamentary Trust? A Testamentary Trust is created by a will. It is set in motion only after the will that creates it is probated. By using a Testamentary Trust, the decedent can provide a legal process or structure by which a trustee can manage the assets, and this has certain benefits. If it's important, a decedent can ensure that children, or other heirs, don't immediately get all of their inheritance. For example, a Testamentary Trust could provide that children receive only the income from the trust until they reach an appropriate age, say 25 or 30, and then get the assets distributed to them free of the trust. The Trust can also be used, if desired, to control assets that will be held in trust for the child's entire life. Having a will with a Testamentary Trust may also save estate taxes. Testamentary Trusts are not used frequently today, because the decedent's assets still go through the probate process. Most people are better off with a trust that stands on its own and doesn't need to go through probate.

CHAPTER 7:

Your Best Option – The Living Trust

Chapter Contents: The 50,000 Foot View of the Living Trust ▶ The Truth About How Trusts Are Written

"Put not your trust in money, but put your money in trust."
Oliver Wendell Holmes (1809–1894)

This Chapter is an overview of a Living (or Revocable) Trust that is often used in modern estate planning. The in-depth issues about the Living Trust are examined in the Chapters that follow.

The 50,000 Foot View of the Living Trust. We return to the bank teller from Chapter 5, who's talking to the nephew of the deceased account owner. If the bank account had been opened as "Uncle Ray, Trustee of the Uncle Ray Trust," rather than just "Uncle Ray's Account," things would have been far easier. No probate, no court order, not even a séance. You would have simply had the customer get a copy of the trust, and see who the trust designated as successor trustee to Uncle Ray. In our example, it would be the nephew. You'd then tell the nephew to get (1) a certified copy of the death certificate, (2) a certified copy of the trust, (3) provide a copy of his, the nephew's, identification, and (4) ask whether he wants cash or a check.

Why did the process suddenly get so easy? The Revocable or Living Trust allows someone to create a legal structure to control their assets both before and after their death. The trust is formed by a legal document and allows the people who create the trust, the trustors or settlors, to enter into a relationship with someone in whom they trust and have confidence. This trusted person, or trustee, takes legal title to the assets and cares for the assets, according to instructions from the trustor, for the benefit of parties identified by the trust as the beneficiaries.

Can the same person be the trustor, the trustee, and a beneficiary? Yes, most Revocable Living Trusts start out this way. The spouses are trustors because they create the trust, trustees because they control the assets during their lives, and beneficiaries because they are entitled to the income and growth from all of the trust assets.

We refer to an estate planning Revocable Trust as a Living Trust because it can be revoked or changed anytime during the settlors' lifetimes, just like a will. One of my clients used to change her will every few months, depending on how well she was getting along with the rest of the family. The same flexibility is built into the Revocable Trust. The Trust can be altered or amended to change which beneficiaries will receive property, to change what property is being given, and to change the terms under which beneficiaries receive property. When the trustors die, the Trust doesn't cease to exist. Instead, under the terms of the Trust, a new trustee takes over, and this trustee holds title to the assets just like the old trustees did before they died.

The Truth About How Trusts Are Written. Because of the forward-looking nature of the Trust, and the uncertainty of life, a well-planned Trust is bulky. It's built the way you build a snowball, made up of lots of tiny bits of information with a very generalized structure. The Living Trust used by a good, contemporary estate planning lawyer has lots of parts that have been added, built up and revised as the tax laws or case law on fiduciary duty have developed and changed. As a result, Living Trusts don't generally read like a novel, or even a well-written business plan. But, correctly drawn, they should protect your assets.

The trustee's duties and tax issues are aspects of trust management which become most difficult as time passes. You may have heard of fiduciary duties. Fiduciary duties are the duties the law imposes on actions by a trustee. At all times, trustees must act in the best interests of the beneficiary, not in their own self-interest. These duties may raise difficult questions for trustees as time passes.

If the trust instrument does not explicitly empower the trustee to deal with certain types of assets, the trustee is put in an awkward position. If the trustee decides to invest in an asset, or even if he continues to hold an asset the trust already contained when he became trustee, he may be sued. If he decides not to invest in or to dispose of the asset, he may be sued. In neither event was the trustee's action explicitly authorized by the trust, and he may therefore be acting outside his instructions, at his peril.

For example, years ago, few trusts explicitly mentioned hazardous waste. Today, however, a trustee may have real property with hazardous waste problems among the assets in the trust. Such a trustee faces a difficult choice. Does he sell the contaminated property or hold it? Similarly, few trusts written long ago explicitly mentioned stock options. What if the trust doesn't mention it, but the assets transferred to a trustee include stock options? Does the trustee have the right to exercise them? Or if he fails to, is he responsible to repay the trust for the profits that might have been made?

I write trusts today that could be in existence for many years, and I have no idea what assets these trusts may someday contain. I put several pages of language in the trust giving the trustee power to deal with many kinds of assets. Many clients get upset when they see this language, because they fear that including this language will encourage the trustee to dabble in dangerous investments. Of course that isn't the intent. The trust instrument contains instructions authorizing the trustee to deal with investment assets as he judges best. This provides the trustee with some measure of protection from being second-guessed or sued.

My own family's trust contains language under which a future trustee could buy or sell real estate and deal with hazardous waste disposal problems, or could exercise, or decline to exercise stock options. This language isn't meant to encourage a trustee to buy stock options for speculation, or to buy superfund cleanup sites. Rather, the empowering language authorizes the trustee to deal, prudently, with specialized assets that the trust may contain at some time. The more things the trustee is authorized to deal with, prudently, the better. That's why my trust has many pages of powers granted to existing and future trustees. I've authorized the trustee to deal with more types of assets than the trust will probably ever contain.

If you, as the person setting up the trust, have a really specific worry that your trustee may implement an investment strategy you disagree with, your trust needs to be a bit longer, not shorter. Rather than cutting out empowering language, and leaving no guidance, the trust language can express the trustor's wishes and intentions very explicitly. Chapter 10 contains in-depth discussion of this, with specific advice about communicating investment preferences and guidance to future trustees.

Every trust will also be affected over time by changes in the tax laws. Right now, the laws are in a tremendous state of flux. Even if they were not, the mix of assets in a trust will change from time to time, which, of course, affects potential tax liability. There's simply no good way to be sure what a trustor's mix of assets will be when that person dies nor what the exact structure of the tax laws will be at that date.

In order to allow the trustee to take the maximum advantage of the tax laws, I put as much flexibility into the trust language as I safely can. Thus, I create trusts with varied instructions for the trustee, and include Sub-Trusts, which are unfunded and exist silently within the main trust while the original trustors are alive. These Sub-Trusts may come into play when one of the trustors dies, depending, of course, on the trust's asset structure and the tax laws in effect at the time of the death.

CHAPTER 8:

The Advantages of
The Living Trust

Chapter Contents: Please Don't Waste Your Tax Exemptions ▶ How The Trust Works ▶ The Survivor's Trust ▶ The Bypass or Credit Shelter Trust ▶ The QTIP or Marital Trust ▶ Putting It All Together For the Basic Estate Plan ▶ Examples of Estate Flow ▶ Summary

"Death is not the final end. There remains the litigation."
Ambrose Bierce (1842–1914)

In this and the following chapters, we'll continue to go into detail about the trust and explain how it can help you avoid any trips to court. First, I'll lay out the trust structure and how it works, then, some of the particular language that can be used. Finally, we'll look at some of the many variations to the Revocable or Living Trust. Understanding the different kinds of advantages that are possible in a Living Trust will help you determine what you need to include in your own Trust.

To understand how it all fits together, though, we need to look at each part Sub-Trust by Sub-Trust, not just asset by asset. The Living Trust is the diamond shaped box in Figure 8-1. While both spouses are alive, the Living Trust is treated as a single trust containing all the family assets, like soup ingredients in one big pot. When one spouse dies, based upon the language of the Living Trust, we split the assets up to fund Sub-Trusts

Estate Flow of Wealth Through Trust Asset by Asset

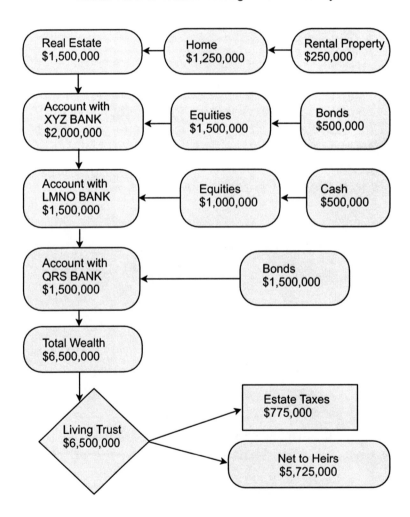

Figure 8-1

Please Don't Waste Your Tax Exemptions. Estate tax exemptions are given to each individual taxpayer. For a couple to avoid paying estate taxes, the first spouse to die could leave half of the family assets directly to the children, rather than the other spouse. If the amount going to the children is less than the estate tax exemption amount of the first spouse, there would be no estate tax on the first death. And when the second spouse dies, those assets would have already passed to the children and won't be in the second spouse's estate.

Although this idea uses the first spouse's exemption amount effectively, it isn't a good plan for practical reasons. The children may be too young to manage or hold property, and the surviving spouse only has access to half the family assets which may not be sufficient for the spouse's needs. There may be other reasons to keep the children's share in trust, which we'll examine in detail in the next several chapters.

How The Trust Works. Let's examine the structure of the assets in a married couple's trust. The following figure shows how assets would flow from different accounts to the Living Trust, then to the heirs.

Figure 8-2, and the accompanying text that follows, explains each Sub-Trust and shows how assets flow. These are sometimes called "A-B" or "ABC" Trusts, and consist of the (1) Survivor's Trust, (2) Bypass or Credit Shelter Trust, and (3) the Marital or QTIP Trust.

Roughly speaking, if our decedent lived in California, and all of the family assets are community property, the assets are split in half. 50% of the assets will go into the Survivor's Trust, and the other 50% are allocated between the Bypass and QTIP Trusts to take full advantage of the estate tax exemption.

Simplified Trust Flow

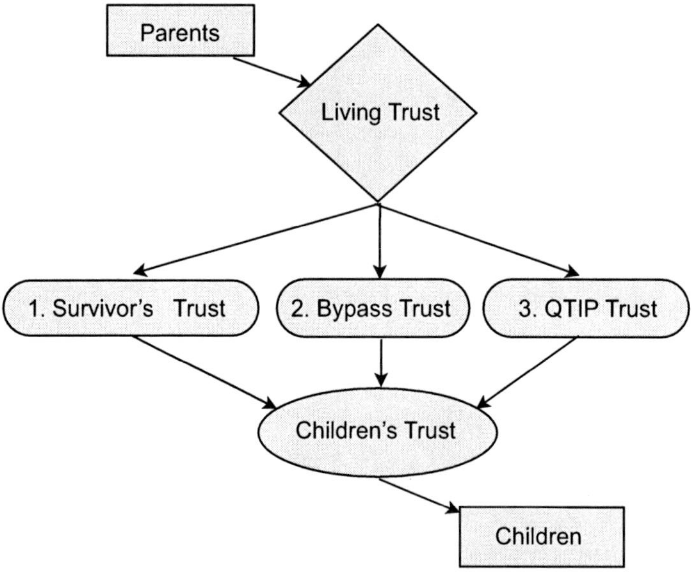

Figure 8-2

The Survivor's Trust. The Survivor's Trust is created to hold the surviving spouse's half of the community property. Assume that all of the family's assets were acquired during marriage and not brought to the marriage by either spouse or acquired through inheritance or gift. In community property states, this entire estate would be considered community property and belong to both spouses equally. Since each spouse owns half of the community property assets, the first spouse to die can give away only his or her half. The survivor retains the rights to his or her half of the assets after the first spouse dies. This half is placed in the Survivor's Trust, and is managed by the survivor for the survivor's benefit and remains in place for the rest of the survivor's life. Much like the original Living Trust, the Survivor's Trust remains revocable, or changeable by the survivor, until the survivor's death.

The Bypass or Credit Shelter Trust. The Bypass Trust does what its name implies. The assets in this trust avoid or bypass the estate tax. They do this by passing over the surviving spouse to a limited extent. Tax laws sometimes refer to the estate tax exemption as the unified credit amount, so the Bypass Trust is sometimes referred to as the Credit Shelter trust since the trust is designed to hold or shelter the estate tax's current exemption amount. Bypass Trust and Credit Shelter Trust are different names for the same Sub-Trust, and I'll use the name Bypass Trust.

After the first spouse's death, assets are allocated to the Bypass Trust in an amount equal to the lifetime federal estate tax exemption for the first spouse. For the Bypass Trust there are two groups of beneficiaries. In the first group is the surviving spouse, who has a life interest in the trust. Having a life interest refers to the right of the surviving spouse to receive all of the income from the trust for the rest of his or her life. The children are typically the second group of beneficiaries, or the remainder beneficiaries. They get whatever property remains in the Bypass Trust after the death of the second spouse.

The Bypass Trust explicitly identifies the children as beneficiaries when it is first funded, giving the children vested rights as remainder beneficiaries at the first death even though they don't get any money until the surviving spouse dies. Under tax rules, these remainder beneficiaries' vested rights are sufficient to make the Bypass Trust subject to the estate tax at the first spouse's death. The first spouse's estate tax exemption is then applied to the assets in the Bypass Trust, so no tax is paid. The Bypass Trust is funded with no more than the amount of the exemption at the time of the first spouse's death. Any extra in the Bypass Trust would create an estate tax liability, at the estate tax rate in effect at the first spouse's death, which is something we are trying to avoid.

Since most families' Survivor's Trust won't contain enough assets to support the surviving spouse securely for the rest of his or her life, the assets placed in the Bypass Trust are held there for the lifetime of the surviving spouse. The surviving spouse's life interest in the Bypass Trust keeps the survivor secure in two ways.

First, the surviving spouse receives all of the income from the Bypass Trust until he or she dies. Second, the survivor may also invade and use the principal from the Bypass Trust in certain circumstances. Usually, this only happens when the assets in the Survivor's Trust are insufficient for the spouse's health, education, maintenance or support.

When the surviving spouse dies, all assets remaining in the Bypass Trust will pass to the children without estate tax. Remember, these assets have already passed through the estate tax system at the time of the first spouse's death. Since we applied the first spouse's exemption to the assets in the Bypass Trust at that date, those assets will pass to the children entirely free of estate tax, regardless of how much they may have gained or appreciated after the death of the first spouse. Paying the income to the surviving spouse during that spouse's lifetime eliminates any potential income tax problems, explained in detail in Chapter 9.

The QTIP or Marital Trust. A QTIP or Marital trust, together with the Bypass Trust, provides the first spouse to die a way to retain control of his or her half of the family property. The term QTIP refers to Qualified Terminable Interest Property. This is also called a Marital Trust. For simplicity, I'll use the term QTIP.

Since the capacity of the Bypass Trust is limited by the amount of the estate tax exemption, the QTIP is needed only in larger estates. An amount equal to the estate tax exemption of the first spouse to die can bypass the estate tax, so that's the maximum amount that's placed into the Bypass Trust on the first death. If the estate is modest in size, half the assets of the family may be less than the capacity of the Bypass Trust. If so, the funding of the trusts is complete. In this case there's no need to fund the QTIP Trust, and it simply gets ignored.

Where the estate contains greater amounts of wealth, there will be assets left over after the Survivor's Trust is funded with half the assets and the Bypass Trust is funded with the exemption amount. This extra amount is placed in the QTIP Trust. Like the Bypass Trust, the surviving spouse usually receives all of the income from the QTIP Trust, and may invade the principal for health, education, maintenance or support. Also like the Bypass Trust, upon the death of the surviving spouse, the property in the QTIP Trust passes to the beneficiaries named by the spouse who died first, usually the children. The QTIP assets won't be subject to estate tax on the first death, but they may be subject to estate tax upon the death of the second spouse depending on the value of the estate.

Putting it All Together for the Basic Estate Plan. Let's plan an estate. We'll assume there's a basic family situation that's fairly simple, with no complications and nothing exotic. See Figure 8-3. This plain vanilla Living Trust avoids the costs and time delays of probate by allowing surviving family members, through their successor trustee, to deal with the assets of the Trust without having to obtain court approval. There will also be a dramatic estate tax savings, as shown in the estate flow charts that follow.

The Typical Family Trust: Estate Plan Flow of Funds

During Your Joint Lifetimes

Joint Revocable Living Trust

During the Trustors' lifetimes, the revocable trust may be amended or revoked. Both owners typically serve as Co-Trustees; if either is unable to serve, the other may be sole Trustee. If neither is able to serve, a Successor Trustee must take over. The income and principal of the Trust are used by the owners as needed for themselves and family, at their complete and sole discretion.

At the First Death

No Tax — *No Tax* — *Tax Deferred*

Survivor's Trust

• Usually Funded w/ 50% of Assets.
• Revocable Trust.
• Survivor is usually the Trustee.
• Survivor/Trustee may use Income or Principal as desired during life.
• Survivor/Trustee may change or revoke terms of Trust during life, just as he or she could with the original Revocable Living Trust.

Bypass Trust

• Funded up to Exclusion Amount. In year 2009, funded with $3.5 Million.
• Irrevocable trust.
• Survivor is usually the Trustee.
• Income Paid to Survivor for Life.
• If Needed, Principal may be invaded for Survivor's Health, Education, Maintenance or Support.
• Remainder usually passes to children at death of Survivor.

QTIP or Marital Trust

• Funded with amounts left after funding the Survivor and Bypass Trusts. [Bypass Trust + QTIP= 50% of total Living Trust assets]
• Irrevocable trust.
• Survivor is usually the Trustee.
• Income Paid to Survivor for Life.
• Remainder usually passes to children at death of Survivor.

Partly Taxable: Tax On Any $ Over Current Exemption Amount — *No Tax* — *Taxable*

At the Second Death

Distributing or Continuing Trusts for Children and/or other Heirs

•Allocated to Children or other Heirs Per Terms of the Sub-Trusts.
•May completely distribute, or may distribute parts at various ages.
•May be split into separate trusts for children, with different rules on distribution.

Figure 8-3

Examples of Estate Flow. The following examples show how the amounts flow through the tax and probate system. Amounts used in the examples are rounded off. The examples are based on 2009 tax rules, as they existed at the beginning of that year, under EGTRRA. Under those rules, there is an exemption amount of $3,500,000. For estates in 2009 that contain assets worth more than the exemption amount of $3,500,000, estate tax must be paid, based upon calculations from a table that starts at a fairly high rate and rapidly rises to the maximum 45% rate. If an estate is worth less than the exemption amount, no estate taxes are due.

In the first example, Figure 8-4, we'll use a brother and sister with no Living Trust and no community property effect. A will is used and the property will pass from Brother to Sister, then from Sister to Sister's Children. The total estate is worth $5,000,000 and both deaths occur in 2009.

Estate Flow Example 1

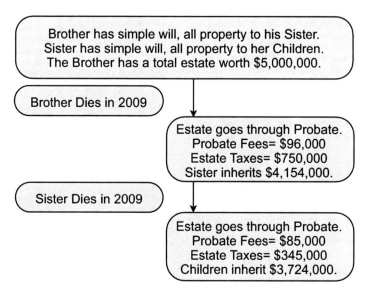

Figure 8-4

The Result: Estate of $5,000,000 is reduced by probate fees totaling $181,000 and estate taxes of $1,095,000. The next generation gets roughly 74% of the original assets.

The imaginary estate in the second example, Figure 8-5, contains community property but does not utilize a Living Trust. This Married couple has simple wills. Property will pass from Husband to Wife, then from Wife to Children. The total estate is worth $5,000,000.

The Result: Estate of $5,000,000 is reduced by probate fees totaling $181,000 and estate taxes of $750,000. The next generation gets roughly 80% of the original assets.

Estate Flow Example 2

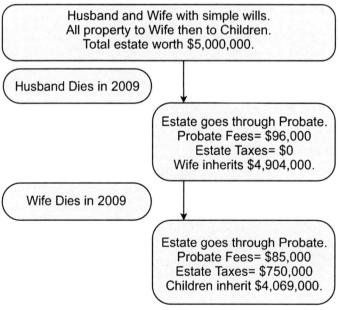

Figure 8-5

In the third example, Figure 8-6, we examine an estate in which the married couple has a Living Trust which has been executed and funded. Property will pass from Husband to Wife, then from Wife to Children. The total estate is worth $5,000,000.

Estate Flow Example 3

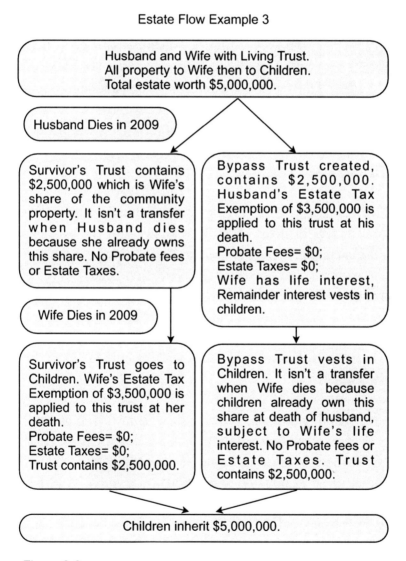

Husband and Wife with Living Trust.
All property to Wife then to Children.
Total estate worth $5,000,000.

Husband Dies in 2009

Survivor's Trust contains $2,500,000 which is Wife's share of the community property. It isn't a transfer when Husband dies because she already owns this share. No Probate fees or Estate Taxes.

Bypass Trust created, contains $2,500,000. Husband's Estate Tax Exemption of $3,500,000 is applied to this trust at his death.
Probate Fees= $0;
Estate Taxes= $0;
Wife has life interest, Remainder interest vests in children.

Wife Dies in 2009

Survivor's Trust goes to Children. Wife's Estate Tax Exemption of $3,500,000 is applied to this trust at her death.
Probate Fees= $0;
Estate Taxes= $0;
Trust contains $2,500,000.

Bypass Trust vests in Children. It isn't a transfer when Wife dies because children already own this share at death of husband, subject to Wife's life interest. No Probate fees or Estate Taxes. Trust contains $2,500,000.

Children inherit $5,000,000.

Figure 8-6

In Example 3, the next generation gets 100% of the original assets.

Notice that in the first example, the children got a bit less than 3/4, or about 74% of the family's assets, after the assets passed through the probate and the tax system after each death.

The second example shows no estate tax liability on the first death, but the lack of a trust still costs the family more than $900,000 in taxes and probate fees. Married couples get a break on community property's first pass through the tax system, so only the second death results in tax liability. In effect, the entire estate passes through the probate system twice and the tax system once, and the children get about 80% of the original family assets passed on to them.

In the third example, with the Living Trust, all of the assets pass without either probate fees or taxes. The Trust allows half the assets to pass through the estate tax system at the first death, using the first spouse's exemption so there's no tax liability on the first death. At the second death, that spouse's exemption is applied to the other half of the assets. By completely utilizing both exemptions there is no tax liability in this third example, and the assets avoid the probate system completely. The children in Example 3 save $1,276,000 over Example 1, and get 100% of the family's assets.

During the planning process, I like to sit with my client and pencil in numbers as if the client finished the plan and died right away. How much do they save? In moderate sized estates it can be $600,000 to $1,000,000, and in larger ones, $2,000,000 to $10,000,000 or more. And these are real, demonstrable tax savings. The day before you sign the estate plan and fund your trusts and the day after are dramatically different from a financial perspective. I frequently say that the time you spend planning your estate often pays off better than any other single job of work you'll do in your life. Ever!

Summary. The tax and probate fee-saving magic is really pretty simple. Break the family trust assets into pieces, with 50% going into the Survivors Trust. Fund the Bypass Trust from the remaining assets, with these assets earmarked to eventually go to the remainder beneficiaries, usually the children. The Bypass Trust uses the first spouse's estate tax exemption. If the estate is larger, half the total assets go in the Survivors Trust, then the Bypass Trust is funded up to the estate tax exemption amount, and any assets left after the Survivors and Bypass Trust are funded go into the QTIP Trust. The QTIP and Bypass Trust will pay income to the surviving spouse and allow the surviving spouse to invade the Trust if the assets are really needed. When the second spouse dies, that spouse's exemption is used on assets in the Survivors Trust. This allows us to fully use each taxpayer's exemption and avoid probate.

CHAPTER 9:

The Life-Cycle of
The Living Trust

Chapter Contents: Life-Cycle of the Trust ▶
How Property is Owned by the Trusts ▶ *Titling
the Assets* ▶ *The Roles in the Trust Structure*
▶ *The Three Stages of Most Trusts* ▶ *After
the Death of the First Trustor* ▶ *Examples
of Funding* ▶ *Tax Aspects* ▶ *Sub-Trusts and
Revocability Changes* ▶ *Allocations of the
Assets in the Sub-Trusts* ▶ *What Goes Where*
▶ *Trust Accounting and the Survivor's Trust*
▶ *Allocation for the Bypass and QTIP Trusts*
▶ *When Both Spouses Die*

"In theory there is no difference between theory and practice.
In practice there is."
Yogi Berra

Life-Cycle of the Trust. Assume that you're now trustee of your Revocable Living Trust. What is it like to live with it? Does the trust complicate your life? Although some aspects of life with a trust require extra care from time to time, most of the management issues are quite easy. On the one hand, you should be managing the trust to maximize the trust's potential tax and financial benefits, and on the other hand, you should keep the management tasks of the trust simple and realistic. Although these activities sometimes conflict, balancing them is the key to effective management of your Trust.

How Property is Owned by the Trust. From a technical, legal perspective, the trustee is the legal owner of the trust assets. The trustee holds title of the trust assets to protect the beneficiary. For example, assume the parents of a small child placed assets in a trust to benefit the child. Assume the parents then pass away. The successor trustee is therefore referred to as the legal owner of the assets, continuing to hold them for benefit of the child, who is referred to as the beneficial owner. In any trust, if there are two or more trustees, actions by joint trustees need to be unanimous unless the trust specifies that one trustee may act alone.

Titling the Assets. There are some steps you must take after the trust is created, and the first step is to fund the trust. Funding the trust has two parts: referring to your assets, either individually or as a group, in the language of the trust document, and re-titling the assets. Re-titling is changing the names under which your assets are held, so that you own them as trustee of your trust, rather than individually. When new assets are purchased, you should take title to them in your name as trustee of your trust. Sometimes you may acquire property in your individual name to satisfy a lender, or for some other reason. Be sure to take the extra step of transferring it to your name as trustee of your trust as soon as you can.

For most trusts, like the one I have for my family, it's easy. The bank checking and savings accounts, investment accounts, and deed to my house have all been changed from 'Judy and Terry Kane' to 'Judy and Terry Kane, Trustees of the Kane Family Trust.' For your reference,

I have posted a sample deed at my website. In some states, including California, real estate is reassessed for property tax purposes when it is transferred, and this often results in increased property taxes. There is a specific exception to this rule for transfers to a Living Trust, so the transfer from owning the property individually to owning it as trustees of our trust has no adverse property tax consequences.

I often refer to the year the trust was signed as part of the title. It isn't essential, but because a trust, like a will, can be changed, or replaced, several times during a person's life, using the year in the title helps to identify the version of the document being used.

I used to go through the process of re-titling all of the assets for my clients, but it gets expensive to have an attorney charge for all of the time it takes to do these changes. With some guidance, most clients have no problem changing names on most of their assets themselves. Of course, your attorney should draft the real estate forms and deeds, and anything complicated. Changing the name on bank accounts and investment accounts is relatively easy for clients to do themselves. Each institution you invest with has its own forms, but they are usually quite simple. Older clients may physically hold individual stock certificates or bonds as investments. In that case, they must send the company issuing the stock certificate or bond a letter instructing them to make the change. There's no reason to change the name on non-probate assets, like retirement accounts, IRAs, and insurance policies, because these assets already have a beneficiary designation. They will automatically go to the person designated without probate.

The Roles in the Trust Structure. In my trust, I have three roles. I'm one of the trustors, one of the trustees, and I'm also one of the beneficiaries. This also is true for my wife as co-trustor, co-trustee and co-beneficiary.

We choose investments and distribute income to ourselves, just as we did before we had our assets in a trust.

The Three Stages of Most Trusts. A trust for a married couple with children typically goes through three stages. The trust is born, or comes into existence, when the trust document is signed. At first, there's a period when both trustors are living, and, during this time, both are usually acting as trustees, and they can do everything with the assets in the plain vanilla Revocable trust that they could've done with the assets before they were acting as trustees.

After the Death of the First Trustor. When one of them dies, the surviving spouse is generally going to be the sole trustee. At that time, that surviving spouse may deal freely with his or her half of the property through the Survivor's Trust. The survivor will get the income from the Bypass and QTIP Sub-Trusts. The survivor also usually has the right to invade the principal of the other Sub-Trusts if the survivor's assets aren't sufficient for the survivor's health, maintenance, or support.

From a tax standpoint, the surviving spouse should take his or her living expenses from the Sub-Trusts' income. If there isn't adequate income, the survivor should generally take principal from the Survivor's Trust first. Then, if allowed by its terms, the surviving spouse should invade the principal of the QTIP Trust next. It makes sense to use these assets first, since the assets in the Survivor's Trust and QTIP Trust have not been taxed at the first death, but may be taxed at the second, depending on the size of the estate.

Invading the Bypass Trust should be avoided. The assets in the Bypass Trust are already being held for the family's children or beneficiaries, and will pass to them at the second spouse's death with no estate tax imposed on them. In fact, if the assets in the Bypass Trust appreciate greatly in value, even more wealth will pass to your children or beneficiaries without being subjected to estate tax.

Examples of Funding. Following are diagrams that illustrate the Sub-Trust funding.

In Figure 9-1, assume the total family's wealth is $4,000,000, and all the assets are community property. The first spouse dies in 2008, when the estate tax exemption amount was $2,000,000. $2,000,000 will be placed in the Bypass Trust, and $2,000,000 in the Survivor's Trust; there's no need to fund a QTIP Trust since there are no remaining assets. At the second spouse's death, the children will get the contents of the Bypass Trust, and if the second spouse hasn't changed the terms of the Survivor's Trust, the children will get the contents of that Sub-Trust as well.

Example of Funding Sub-Trusts

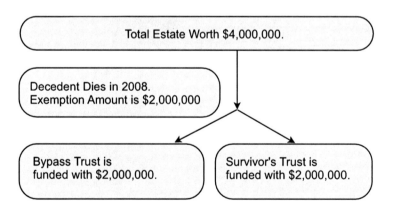

Figure 9-1

In Figure 9-2, assume, again, that the total family wealth is $4,000,000, all community property, but the first spouse died in 2005, when the exemption was $1,500,000. The Bypass Trust would be funded with $1,500,000. The Survivor's Trust would contain half of the family wealth, or $2,000,000. The remaining $500,000 would be placed in the QTIP Trust at the death of the first spouse. The surviving spouse can't change the final disposition of the property in either the Bypass Trust, or in the QTIP Trust. This follows the intention of the deceased spouse, and protects the children, or other beneficiaries, of the original family. It also protects the surviving spouse by allowing the spouse to use the income, and, if necessary, the principal of the trust.

Example of Funding Sub-Trusts

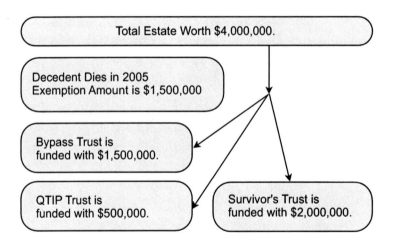

Figure 9-2

Tax Aspects. While the trust is revocable and at least one of the trustors is acting as a trustee, a Living Trust is not required to file a tax return or have a tax identification number. As time passes, if none of the original trustor is a trustee, the successor trustee must apply for a tax identification number, which is the same as an employer identification number, and file tax returns.

However, upon the death of one of the spouses, the tax aspects of Living Trusts change. Once it's funded, each irrevocable Sub-Trust becomes a separate tax reporting entity which needs to get a tax identification number, file a tax return, and, if necessary, make tax payments.

Each trust reports the income it has received on its tax return, but if all of its income is distributed, the trust gets a deduction for the entire amount of distributed income. This means there's no actual tax liability at the trust level. The information from the trust's tax return is reported on the personal return of the life beneficiary, that is, the spouse, and any income tax is paid when the money reaches that life beneficiary. For just this reason, distribution of the net income is usually required by the terms of the trust. In theory, it's possible for trust income to be taxed to the trust as an entity, then again to the recipient on their personal tax return. However, with proper structure of the trust, assets, and cash flow, there won't be double taxation.

Sub-Trusts and Revocability Changes. The structure of the Sub-Trusts become much more important in post-death management. When one spouse dies, the revocability of parts of the trust change. The Bypass and QTIP Trusts become irrevocable after the first death. Most people structure their trust this way for control reasons. The surviving spouse may remarry, and the surviving spouse's hypothetical new partner may have children as well. Using this Bypass and QTIP Trust mechanism, the first spouse to die knows that the children of their marriage will get at least that spouse's half of the community property. The new partner of a surviving spouse will not be able to divert this portion of the estate from the deceased trustors' children.

Allocation of the Assets in the Sub-Trusts. In order to allocate assets, we must (1) value, (2) divide, and (3) re-title the assets or accounts. This is done so the trusts will have the best balance of cash flow and growth, tax advantage and ease of administration.

The actual physical separation and allocation of the assets isn't done by painting a line down the middle of the room, although they sometimes did it this way on old "I Love Lucy" episodes. The allocation or division is done by changing the title to the assets into the name of the specific Sub-Trust, and/or by identification and treatment of the asset in the accounting records of the trust. The assets of the Sub-Trusts may be treated as a unit, for ease of management, if the Sub-Trusts so authorize. For accounting purposes, the assets must still be accounted for separately for each Sub-Trust.

Example: Suppose your trust owns half of the family plumbing business. The business is organized as a corporation, and ownership is evidenced by stock certificates. If it would be advantageous that some shares be placed into the Bypass Trust, the trustee requests that the corporate secretary cancel the existing shares and issue retitled ones in appropriate amounts. On the face of the new shares, they are owned by "Terry and Judy Kane as Trustees of the Terry and Judy Kane Bypass Trust."

What Goes Where. We've been examining the process of dividing the Living Trust into two or three separate Sub-Trusts when one of the trustors dies. As we've seen, the Survivor's Trust is allocated assets equal to half of the community property, and usually all of the surviving Trustor's separate property. Assets equal to the estate tax exemption are allocated to the Bypass Trust. The remainder of the property is allocated to the QTIP Trust.

The trustee oversees the process of determining the value of the assets, and then divides or allocates the assets. The trustee is guided by the trust document's provisions, and acts with an eye to getting the most advantage possible for the beneficiaries. Sometimes, an asset is allocated, in parts, to more than one trust. For example, half of the house could be owned by the trustee for the Bypass Trust, and the other half for the Survivor's Trust. Most trust documents I draft also permit the trustee to place whole assets, and not just parts, into the Sub-Trusts if this would be beneficial. Whether or not this is ultimately done depends on the present and future needs of the beneficiaries, as seen by the trustee.

Example: Suppose the family home is originally held by the Living Trust. Upon the first spouse's death, the trustee could allocate it partly to the Bypass Trust, the QTIP, and the Survivor's Trust, or the trustee could allocate it entirely to only one of the Sub-Trusts.

Choice 1. In some family situations, allocation of the entire family home to the Survivor's Trust is psychologically important for the surviving spouse's peace of mind. The surviving spouse feels an increase in security, because the survivor now has total control over the home. Total control over an asset is a two-edged sword, however. Since the survivor can now control the management and disposition of the family home entirely, the survivor could change the way in which the home is ultimately disposed of. This may be contrary to the wishes of the deceased spouse.

Choice 2. In other families, the house could be placed in the Bypass Trust and an equal value of assets can be placed in the Survivor's Trust. Since homes often appreciate greatly in value over time, this may place an asset with the highest potential growth in the most tax protected portion of the trust. No matter how much the assets in the Bypass Trust appreciate, there will be no estate tax imposed on them upon the death of the second spouse. This can, however, have a less beneficial effect from a capital gains perspective. The Bypass Trust assets avoid estate tax completely, but the basis for those assets will be the value at the death of the first spouse, not the second. This means a portion of the capital gains taxes are delayed, but in the Survivor's Trust, capital gains taxes on the same asset would be forgiven. The basis for assets held in the Survivor's Trust will be the market value at the second spouse's death.

As you can see, there's no single rule that governs the decision of where to place the family home. Much depends on what the trustor thinks will happen in the long run.

At the death of a trustor, the trust assets must be valued, for at least two reasons. First, estate taxes are based on the current market value of assets, and estate tax returns must be filed if there are taxable amounts in the trust. Second, assets must be allocated to the proper Sub-Trusts based upon the current value. This is a task that your lawyer should help you perform, usually, along with a tax accountant and perhaps an appraiser. If you've read other books on planning, they may have made this sound difficult or complicated. It does require some expertise, but it's far simpler than the effort required to go through probate when there is no Living Trust. What you, as trustee, can do to make this process go smoothly is to keep good records of expenses and assets.

Under the tax law, the trustee can elect to use the date of death as the date for valuing the assets, or choose a date six months after the death. Generally, most trustees wait until the six months has passed, to see if the values changed in a favorable way. At that time, they make the choice of dates for valuing the assets.

Trust Accounting and Allocation for the Survivor's Trust. After the death of one of the spouses, the Survivor's Trust continues to have many attributes the Living Trust had when both spouses were alive. Specifically, the rules for taxation and the rules for changing the trust are just like the rules which applied to the entire Living Trust when both spouses were around.

Allocation for the Bypass and QTIP Trusts. There's a new accounting issue for the Bypass and QTIP Trusts when the first spouse dies. You needn't fear the complexities if you are to act as trustee, but you need to recognize that they exist and keep track of them accordingly.

When both spouses were alive, they had the right to the income and principal of the trust. When there's a death, the surviving spouse is usually the income or life beneficiary of the Bypass and QTIP Trusts, and the children are usually the remainder beneficiaries. The accounting and legal rules require the trustee to allocate income and expense properly.

For example, amounts received from trust assets are recorded as income or principal, and are allocated either entirely for one trust or split into parts and allocated between several Sub-Trusts. Expenses to the trust may relate to income or principal, or to both, and a single payment can have many different components. The sale of an asset may result in return of the principal used to buy the asset and income related to earnings from the asset, received as a single check.

When one person is the only beneficiary of a trust, it really doesn't matter how the payment gets classified. When one beneficiary gets the income, and a different beneficiary will get the remainder of the original assets, it's important to accurately recognize the character of payments or expenses. The Uniform Principal and Income act, which is the law in California and many other states, provides guidance for these allocations. In addition, language of the trust document may provide guidance or may give the trustee discretion to determine the manner of allocation of payments to the trust as principal or income.

Computing correct allocations of trust expenses can be a fairly complicated exercise. Certain types of debts, such as real estate loans or liens for taxes on the real estate, are related to the particular asset in question. In that case, the asset and the debt should be allocated together. Personal debts, like unpaid bills of the deceased spouse, may be apportioned against all of the trust estate, or may be allocated to different Sub-Trusts depending upon the nature of the debt. A trustee needs to be careful when allocating trust assets, and may need to consult a lawyer or an accountant who understands trust accounting.

This process shouldn't be cumbersome or mysterious, but there are detailed laws as well as the language of the trust itself to consider. When any question about an allocation issue comes up, don't guess. Ask your lawyer or your accountant. This complexity is a reason many clients use a bank trust department or professional fiduciary to act as trustee. Professional fiduciaries deal with these issues frequently and develop expertise and sensitivity to the issues which may be involved.

When Both Spouses Die. When both trustors have died, in the case of a married couple, the entire trust becomes irrevocable as did the Bypass and QTIP Trusts on the first spouse's death. If the beneficiaries are competent adults, and the trust specifies it, the only role of the trustee may be final distribution. In such a case the trustee's job is to pay out the assets and terminate the trust. However, other trusts continue in existence for long periods of time, if there are ongoing trust issues for children, for example, with different needs.

CHAPTER 10:

Living Trust Management, Part 1

Chapter Contents: Building a Team of Professionals ▶ A Trust Should Be Personalized ▶ Duration of the Trust ▶ Investment Strategy and Controls ▶ Building Character in Heirs ▶ A Traditional Example: The Spendthrift Trust ▶ A Complex Example: The Special Needs Trust ▶ An Exotic Example: The Pet Trust ▶ Possessions and Lists ▶ How Many Decisions Do You Need to Make In Advance?

Client: "A friend recommended you.
He said you're a very good lawyer."

Groucho: "You only think he's your friend."

From the Marx Brothers Radio program,
Flywheel, Shyster & Flywheel

[Note: You probably don't actually want
to take legal advice from Groucho Marx.]

Building a Team of Professionals. Before we explore the details of managing your trust, it's good to remember you need not face any of the questions we'll explore alone. Your peace of mind is very important, so when any of the issues in managing your trust cause you uncertainty, seek help from professional advisors. You need a team, and you need to know how to work with them. Learning how a good team is assembled and who needs to be on it is our next step.

I was raised in a small town, where everyone has a reputation, whether good or bad. If you consult the right people, you can find out what you need to know about anyone in a small town. Even in big cities, accountants, lawyers and financial advisors operate in communities that are very similar to small towns. The best tend to know each other and to know those to avoid.

To assemble a team of qualified experts, start with the person you've got the best relationship with already, and have them help you build your team. Got a good CPA? Ask if they have a good financial advisor they'd recommend working with. Don't know how to select a fiduciary, an accountant or a financial advisor? Need an institutional trustee? Call me, or your own family lawyer if you have one. The best team is one that already works together, or at least knows each other by reputation, so there's higher compatibility from the start.

A Trust Should Be Personalized. The wants and needs of your family must be the major focus of any successful structure used for wealth management, asset preservation and estate planning. For most families, the biggest concern is holding their assets safely and distributing them according to their desires. Because these wants and needs vary greatly, there truly isn't a one-size-fits-all answer for a trust. Since you are the one most familiar with your family situation, you can best decide which strategies to implement.

For example, do you have minor children to care for? If so, you and your spouse need to figure out and agree on their guardians and how they will be cared for. You know your children's ability to handle money, and you are the best people to decide whether your children get the trust assets outright when they reach legal majority, or have the assets distributed to them later. Do you have particular assets that you really want to earmark for a particular beneficiary? Do you have strong preferences in terms of investments that should or should not be made with the assets in your trust? Your desires are what the estate plan is all about. You need to learn about your options, think about your goals and communicate these desires. Once you understand what tools are available to you, then you and your lawyer can select the best tools and strategies, and make them part of your plans.

Duration of the Trust. How long can your trust conceivably last? In the abstract, you have a wide range of possibilities. What's best for you depends on your needs and your situation and on what the law will allow. There are some states, such as Alaska or Nevada, which allow long term trusts, and others, such as South Dakota and Delaware which allow perpetual trusts. In most states, though, there's a legal limitation on the lifespan of a trust called the rule against perpetuities. It's simple as a concept but often difficult to apply to particular cases. The rule states that you can't make a trust that never ends and ties up your assets forever.

From a philosophical point of view, I agree with laws that place a limit on the lifespan of a trust. Your foresight probably isn't so clear that all of your progeny should be required to follow your choices to the end of recorded time. Your great-grandchildren might have good ideas about things they'd like to do with whatever's left of your estate, and a long-term plan that ties up assets indefinitely might prevent something wonderful from happening.

On the other hand, some people with large estates want to ensure their family legacy's safety as a paramount concern and have definite ideas on how this should be done over a very long span of time. In such a case, a Legacy Trust can be used to keep the trust from ever distributing the assets outright to the heirs. This way the heirs can't change the plans for the original assets.

There's also a financial plus to a Legacy Trust. Some tax burdens and expenses strike only when property passes from generation to generation. Ownership of the property in a Legacy Trust never legally passes to the beneficiaries. Because the assets remain in the trust, with beneficiaries only entitled to trust income while they live, the Legacy Trust gets a tax advantage. Over several generations, the tax savings can be impressive assuming that the tax laws stay the same. This legacy concept appeals greatly to clients who are very tax-averse or who have a family fortune that is part of their identity. It is not a good idea for those who want simplicity in management, because a trust with a lengthy lifespan needs to be very explicit and thorough.

Investment Strategy and Controls. If you have opinions about the propriety of particular investments or activities, be sure to include information about this in the language of your trust. If you have moral objections to certain investment opportunities, you might implement Socially Responsible Investing. SRI can include making sure that there's no investment of family assets in a country or group of countries where there are important political differences. SRI investing can be used where the client thinks certain kinds of behavior and the companies that profit from them should be avoided from a moral standpoint. For example, some clients are opposed to holding assets in sin stocks like tobacco and firearms companies. SRI investing can also be used to select investments, where clients are proponents of environmentally progressive or green companies. If these issues are important to you, you should address SRI with your investment advisor and make it a part of your overall plan.

Building Character in Heirs. Many wealthy clients worry less about leaving their heirs the biggest dollar amount they possibly can and more about whether too much wealth will wreck their children. Would a $50 million inheritance ruin the character of your child, creating an irresponsible trust fund baby? If you feel it could, you can try to protect your heirs. Often, wealthy parents leave only part of their assets to their children, and leave the rest in a family foundation, a nonprofit organization, or another vehicle that benefits the community. These clients may appoint the children as directors of the family foundation. If the children have the task of helping to specify what organizations or causes benefit from the family's wealth, important moral values, and not just assets, can get passed from parents to the next generation.

Here are more examples of how your trust can be personalized, ranging from traditional, to complex, to exotic:

A Traditional Example: The Spendthrift Trust. Imagine that one of your children can't manage money. If you're concerned that an unsophisticated, immature or careless child would squander property left to them, you might want to use language that creates a spendthrift trust for their protection. Spendthrift language may be inserted in your trust to severely limit or restrict what the beneficiary can do. With such language, your beneficiary can't sell, borrow against, or otherwise get an advance on their share, beyond what the trust will permit. Without this language, the beneficiary, who is only entitled to income from the trust, may be able to borrow against the underlying trust assets or pledge his right to income to a creditor in exchange for a lump sum payment.

A Complex Example: The Special Needs Trust. Suppose that a disabled beneficiary needs medical help, and will continue to need this type of help for his entire life. A special needs trust can set up an investment management structure to protect him. This beneficiary may be completely incapable of making financial decisions so having decisions made by a trusted person is a practical necessity. From a legal perspective, the beneficiary of the trust may be getting financial assistance from a government program. If a person has too many assets, they may no longer qualify for assistance. In such a case, placing ownership in the name of the trustee, not the beneficiary, keeps the beneficiary from owning the assets. At the same time, it fills the need to have a trusted person manage the assets for the beneficiary. Setting up and administering a special needs trust is a very exacting and difficult task that involves following many complex rules and should not be attempted without an attorney who specializes in this area of law.

An Exotic Example: The Pet Trust. Suppose a pet lover wants to leave her kitten millions of dollars. In most states, a cat can't legally own any money (dogs can't either). However, there's a technique to make sure pets are taken care of. By law, a pet is considered property and can't own money. However, a person can be given the pet and can be given some money to care for it. I structure the trust of a concerned pet owner to leave the pet to a trustworthy caretaker along with funds to provide for it.

Possessions and Lists. What about your personal treasures? Again, there's no single right answer. What you need to do depends on your comfort level. Some people have very definite ideas about where particular items must go: 'Make sure my piano goes to my cousin, and my locket must go to my niece.' These people need to incorporate instructions about possessions as part of their plan. Other people have no concern about their furnishings and belongings. They can simply let their successor trustee, or their children, make the division after they're gone. Which path you choose for your heirs is, again, up to you. My own rule of thumb is very practical: Will you lose sleep worrying about what will happen after death to certain things you own, or worrying about causing disagreements among your children? If so, you need to make a list, and the information from that list should be part of your estate plan.

As your life changes, you will acquire new things and get rid of old ones. A list that contains some of your important items but omits others could cause trouble. Worse trouble could be caused by a list that refers to items you no longer have at the time of your death. Those who survive you will try to follow your wishes, and they may have considerable anxiety trying to find assets that you have disposed of but that weren't crossed off your list. If the specific distribution of your personal assets is important to you, you will need to make updates whenever there's a change in those assets.

How Many Decisions Do You Need To Make In Advance? As trustor, many other things are within your power to direct, and the successor trustee has the obligation to follow the trustor's directions. When the directions are clear and there's no change of circumstances, following explicit directions is simple. Of course, a trustor can't give explicit directions on every possible decision a successor trustee could ever make. You've selected this successor trustee because of the faith you, the trustor, have in that trustee to make decisions you would approve of. If the trust doesn't explicitly deal with the exact situation, then the trustee is to do what the trustor would have wanted, using his or her best judgment.

CHAPTER 11:

Living Trust Management, Part 2

Chapter Contents: Successor Trustees: How Many do You Need? ▶ *Successor Trustees: Who Should You Choose?* ▶ *Paying the Trustee or Not* ▶ *Compensation* ▶ *Powers of the Trustees* ▶ *Standards For Management* ▶ *Duty to Report* ▶ *Multiple Roles* ▶ *The Uniform Principal and Income Act* ▶ *Proper Care of Trust Assets* ▶ *QDOT for the Foreign National* ▶ *Exercise Caution*

"Annual income twenty pounds, annual expenditure nineteen six, result happiness. Annual income twenty pounds, annual expenditure twenty pound ought and six, result misery."

David Copperfield, Charles Dickens
(1812–1870)

Successor Trustees: How Many do You Need? It isn't technically necessary to name any successor trustees. The trust will not fail in any legal sense without successors being named. You have the power to add terms to your trust, including nominating additional trustees later. Since it's statistically rare for both spouses to die simultaneously, the surviving spouse will probably be around to select a successor at a later date, and even if no successor is ever named, the court can appoint one.

In practice, I always recommend naming at least one successor trustee. After all, part of good planning is peace of mind. Since it isn't inconceivable that your first choice may not be available, I usually suggest that clients also select a successor to the successor. What about a successor to the successor's successor? Some clients compile a list that's ten, fifteen or even twenty names long. If it's comforting to them, then I use it, but it's probably overkill. If you and your first nineteen alternates all die suddenly, chances are that it was a cataclysmic event. The meteor shower that got your first nineteen choices probably got your twentieth, too, and also destroyed all of your assets! At some point, you have to stop worrying.

Successor Trustees: Who Should You Choose? Who should your successor trustee be? This depends on what you want and need the trustee to do. Good sense is the primary requirement of any trustee. Familiarity with your family and financial sensibilities that are similar to yours are also good qualities. The successor does not need to be an accountant or a lawyer, but it's important that the successor be a person who understands, and will be able to carry out, what you have in mind.

Sometimes, your family situation indicates that you need a successor trustee with a very strong personality. For example, if one of your beneficiaries has emotional or financial difficulties, they may seek to manipulate any family member who is trustee. Worse, if some of your beneficiaries hate each other, the person you select as successor trustee will be put in the middle of the fight to come. In that case, a professional trustee from a major trust company or bank may be a far better choice than a family member.

When do you need an institutional or professional trustee? Some of your family members might find the job of trustee overwhelming. If you don't have a family member or close friend who can be independent and be careful with your assets after you're gone, a bank trust department or professional fiduciary can serve these functions. Banks, trust companies and private fiduciaries bring many capabilities and attributes to the job of trustee. The most obvious advantage to your estate will be the expertise, objectivity and the longevity of the professional organization itself. As our population ages, I frequently see clients outlive their chosen successor trustees, but they won't outlive a solid bank or trust company.

A professional trustee will help assess and review the trust itself, making sure you and the trustee agree on what you wish to accomplish through your estate and asset management plans. He or she will be more experienced about management and more committed than an amateur so the implementation of your plan should go more smoothly. In addition, detailed record keeping, administration, reporting and collection of interest and dividends, the calculation of gains and losses, and tax preparation are important tasks that a non-professional trustee may find daunting. For a professional trustee, these are normal daily activities. The professional trustee you choose needs to have experience, be responsive to your wishes, and be with an organization that is substantial enough to manage your assets with a long term commitment to the trust process.

Paying the Trustee or Not. Trustees do many kinds of tasks when they manage a trust, but most fall within two distinct types. One type of task is to manage existing trust assets as required under the law and the terms of the trust, called trust management. Trust management includes collecting and disbursing income, paying expenses, reporting to the beneficiaries and filing tax returns. Another type of task is to manage and invest the trust assets themselves, called investment management. Investment management includes periodically re-evaluating the trust's existing assets, deciding what assets to keep, and what assets to sell and reinvest differently.

Professional trustees charge fees for their services, usually based upon a percentage of the assets they manage. Sometimes a trust will specify the amount or formula for compensation. Some professionals quote an all inclusive rate that does not itemize the different activities the trustee undertakes. Others separate the fees for trust management from the fees for investment management. The investment management fees may also vary with the types of assets. For example, managing a portfolio of long term bonds may be less active, and therefore cheaper, than managing a stock portfolio with short term and long term investments.

In general, about one and a half to two percent of the principal balance of the trust, per annum, is appropriate for combined investment and trust management services. Institutional trustees who itemize trust services separately generally charge about .1% to .2%, added to their other investment management fees. The investment management services of a professional often create more value for your trust than they cost. If you have great financial managers at work, they will provide a safe and productive blend of assets. These will get a better, more consistent, and safer return for the trust. The fee being charged may, in many cases, be far less than the extra value derived from professional management.

If there are now two conflicting ideas in your mind, it's understandable. First, you'd like a family member as trustee, someone with continuing, family connections and depth of knowledge about personal matters.

But you'd also like the objectivity and professionalism of a professional trustee. Don't overlook the possibility of getting both at the same time, by having a family member and a professional act as co-trustees.

Compensation. A trustee is entitled to reasonable compensation for services performed for the trust. Family members are often picked as trustee because the trustor thinks that they'll work for free. After all, the trustor thinks, it's all in the family. However, if there's substantial work involved managing the trust, this really isn't appropriate or fair.

A trustee never chooses a wasteful or inattentive child or relative to act as trustee. If a diligent, sensible child or relative is made trustee, then they're doing work that takes time and for which they experience opportunity cost. Opportunity cost refers to the fact that they could be doing something else, and getting paid for it, with the time they spend as trustee. So acting as trustee for free is a cost to them. Rather than burdening a family member with managing a trust for free, it's often a better idea to pay the trustee, whether the trustee is a family member or not. Paying the family member trustee acknowledges that there is value to the work this person must do, and will ensure that the trustee is willing and able to spend the time necessary to do a good job.

Powers of the Trustees. In Chapter 7, I discussed the forward-looking aspect of trust language, and how the powers of the trustees are set out in the trust document, sometimes in mind-numbing detail. Trusts generally give the trustees broad powers to deal with problems. The actual use or application of these powers is usually straightforward. Purely clerical functions, such as trust accounting work may be delegated to others by the trustee. The trustee must not delegate his duty to oversee and review the work of others, however. Discretionary decisions, particularly discretionary trust distributions to beneficiaries, should always be made by the trustee, and should not be delegated.

Standards for Management. The trustee is required, by law, to manage assets of the trust as a prudent person would do. The difference between this standard and what you'd do for your own property, for example, is explained in the next paragraphs.

While acting as trustee, there's no reason to agonize over a question about the extent of the power you have. If your authorization is not clear from the express terms of the trust, contact your attorney. If your attorney is unable to provide a clear answer, a petition for instructions may be filed with the Probate Department of the Superior Court, and the court will make the trustee's duty clear. By the way, this doesn't create a situation in which the entire estate must be probated, and therefore subject to excessive delay and additional fees. It's a single motion in front of the probate court, usually resolved in 30 to 90 days.

Duty to Report. Absent trust language to the contrary, a trustee is under a duty to report to the beneficiaries. The trustee is usually required to furnish the beneficiaries of a trust with an annual accounting; however, this can vary, depending on the directions in the trust. This accounting shows, at minimum, the starting balance of trust assets, the income or gain, expenses or losses, and the final balance at the end of the period. Some trusts have very elaborate rules on reporting to beneficiaries; I usually draft trusts so that the reporting to the beneficiaries is as simple and straightforward as possible.

Multiple Roles. A trustee has a fiduciary duty to the beneficiaries of the trust. Recall that the trustee will have taken legal title to the assets. 'Terry and Judy Kane as Trustees of the Kane Family Trust' is what my deed now recites. As trustee I'm the legal owner of the trust assets, and the beneficiaries are the beneficial owners. In other words, the trustee owns the property for the beneficiaries' benefit and not his own. Of course, while my wife and I both live, we're trustees, trustors, and also the primary beneficiaries. Our trust explicitly states that we can do whatever we want with our assets at this stage.

When one of us dies, the Bypass Trust and QTIP trust have the children as remainder beneficiaries and the surviving spouse as income beneficiary and as trustee. The interests of income and remainder beneficiaries are not identical, since one benefits from immediate income return from the trust assets, while the other benefits from growth of those assets. The trustee must administer the trust for all the beneficiaries, in accordance with the intention of the trustor, the terms of the trust agreement, and the standards set by law. By law, the trustee is held to the standard of a prudent investor. What this means, in practical terms, is that there needs to be income for the income beneficiaries to use, but safeguards to preserve the principal are even more important.

Example: Suppose you own, outside of trust, a commercial property which has a building on it. The building will require maintenance over time and will eventually become obsolete. From an accounting standpoint, you should be setting aside amounts out of income for the repair and eventual replacement of the asset. Suppose, however, that you didn't set aside any funds as reserves on this property. As sole owner, this is a choice you can freely make, and you'll have to raise the money to repair and replace the building some other way. It may not have been wise, but you won't sue yourself. If the building is held in a trust, then it's expected that a portion of the building income be set aside as a 'reserve' by the trustee. As the building ages, it is being used up. Without reserves to pay for repair and replacement, the interests of the remainder beneficiaries are harmed.

The terms of the trust may authorize a trustee not to establish a reserve if that's the trustor's intent. Trusts may even authorize the trustee to retain certain assets although they produce no income. The family home, for example, isn't usually rented to anyone, it's occupied by family members. With appropriate language in the trust, letting the family members stay rent free is not a breach of duty by the trustee.

Where the interests of the trustee and any of the beneficiaries aren't identical, all actions taken by the trustee with regard to the trust must be with the best interest of the beneficiaries in mind. The trustee cannot deal with the trust assets in a way that puts the personal benefit of the trustee over the best interests of the beneficiaries. Self-dealing, as the law refers to it, is a breach of trust.

The most likely situation in which self-dealing arises is where the trustee is buying assets from the trust or selling assets to the trust. There's a red flag here even if the beneficiaries also profit from the transaction because the trustee can be accused of having mixed motives. (1) A trustee can transfer assets in and out of a trust, even if the trustee is also one of the beneficiaries, but caution must be exercised to make sure the transaction is in the best interest of all of the beneficiaries. (2) A trustee should not only avoid self dealing, but even the appearance of self-dealing. (3) For very important transactions, the trustee can seek court approval of a proposed transaction in advance.

The Uniform Principal and Income Act. Investments of a trust are evaluated according to the standards set forth in the Trust document, the case law, and the statutory standards set forth in the Uniform Principal and Income Act. This is the law in many jurisdictions. In California, it is contained in Probate Code Sections 16335 et seq. The Act provides, in part:

16335. (a) In allocating receipts and disbursements to or between principal and income, and with respect to any other matter within the scope of this chapter, a fiduciary:

(1) Shall administer a trust or decedent's estate in accordance with the trust or the will, even if there is a different provision in this chapter. ...

(b) In exercising a discretionary power of administration ... the fiduciary shall administer the trust or decedent's estate impartially, except to the extent that the trust or the will expresses an intention that the fiduciary shall or may favor one or more of the beneficiaries. The exercise of discretion in accordance with this chapter is presumed to be fair and reasonable to all beneficiaries.

If the proposed acts of a trustee are being scrutinized to see if there's a breach of duty, examination of the specific language of the trust is required to see if the action the trustee seeks to take is within the trustee's discretionary authority under the trust language.

Investments made by the trustee must comply with both the instructions in the trust and the Probate Code:

16040. (a) The trustee shall administer the trust with reasonable care, skill, and caution under the circumstances then prevailing that a prudent person acting in a like capacity would use in the conduct of an enterprise of like character and with like aims to accomplish the purposes of the trust as determined from the trust instrument. ...

16041. A trustee's standard of care and performance in administering the trust is not affected by whether or not the trustee receives any compensation. ...

16046. (a) Except as provided in subdivision (b), a trustee who invests and manages trust assets owes a duty to the beneficiaries of the trust to comply with the prudent investor rule.

(b) The settlor may expand or restrict the prudent investor rule by express provisions in the trust instrument. A trustee is not liable to a beneficiary for the trustee's good faith reliance on these express provisions.

16047. (a) A trustee shall invest and manage trust assets as a prudent investor would, by considering the purposes, terms, distribution requirements, and other circumstances of the trust. In satisfying this standard, the trustee shall exercise reasonable care, skill, and caution.

(b) A trustee's investment and management decisions respecting individual assets and courses of action must be evaluated not in isolation, but in the context of the trust portfolio as a whole and as a part of an overall investment strategy having risk and return objectives reasonably suited to the trust.

(c) Among circumstances that are appropriate to consider in investing and managing trust assets are the following, to the extent relevant to the trust or its beneficiaries:

    (1)   General economic conditions.

    (2)   The possible effect of inflation or deflation.

    (3)   The expected tax consequences of investment decisions or strategies.

    (4)   The role that each investment or course of action plays within the overall trust portfolio.

    (5)   The expected total return from income and the appreciation of capital.

(6) Other resources of the beneficiaries known to the trustee as determined from information provided by the beneficiaries.

(7) Needs for liquidity, regularity of income, and preservation or appreciation of capital. An asset's special relationship or special value, if any, to the purposes of the trust or to one or more of the beneficiaries.

(d) A trustee shall make a reasonable effort to ascertain facts relevant to the investment and management of trust assets.

(e) A trustee may invest in any kind of property or type of investment or engage in any course of action or investment strategy consistent with the standards of this chapter.

16048. In making and implementing investment decisions, the trustee has a duty to diversify the investments of the trust unless, under the circumstances, it is prudent not to do so. ...

16051. Compliance with the prudent investor rule is determined in light of the facts and circumstances existing at the time of a trustee's decision or action and not by hindsight.

A trustee must keep his own property separate from trust property. Commingling a trustee's own property with the trust property can lead, rather quickly, to claims of self-dealing.

Proper Care of Trust Assets. Trustees must care for the assets of the trust. If you have intrinsically valuable assets, like certificates for stocks and bonds, please put them in a safe place. Most folks select a home safe or a safe deposit box. I know of instances where the trustee was surprised to find a large sum in gold coins hidden behind a panel in the closet and ten thousand dollars cash in the trunk of an old car.

The obvious danger from hidden assets is the possibility they'll be stolen. There's also a danger that the trustee will unknowingly sell the house, or car, with these unknown assets still concealed in them. If you must conceal an asset to protect your family, please leave some kind of written record of it in a safe place or with someone you trust.

You probably have insurance on your most valuable assets, so when you are in the process of changing the name on the assets, contact your insurance company or broker, and add your name, in your role as trustee of your family trust, as a named insured party under the policy.

QDOT for the Foreign National. As we saw in Chapter 8, our current tax laws are very favorable to a surviving spouse, because the transfer to a spouse after the first death is estate tax free. Usually, the assets are taxed after the death of the surviving spouse if the estate is large enough. Congress feared that if the surviving spouse is not a U.S. citizen, property could be removed from U.S. estate tax jurisdiction to a foreign country by the surviving spouse, and the entire estate would escape U.S. Estate Tax. To prevent this, the tax laws provide that when the surviving spouse is not a U.S. Citizen, there is no tax-free passage of wealth from the first spouse to the second unless certain requirements are met. To avoid a tax burden at the first death, language must be drafted into the Living Trust so that it qualifies as a QDOT, or Qualified Domestic Trust. The requirements are fairly technical, but the main practical effect is that a U.S. fiduciary, typically a Bank or Trust company, must serve as the trustee, which will limit the ability of the non-citizen spouse to move the assets overseas to avoid tax.

Exercise Caution. I have defended a number of trustees in lawsuits in which they were accused of acting improperly. In such cases, if the trustees had been found to be negligent, they could have been surcharged or fined for that negligence. Consider the implications of this carefully when you act as trustee. I don't want to discourage you unnecessarily from being your own trustee, or from being trustee for your family members. However, first consider the risks intelligently. Are the trust's beneficiaries closely related to you and well known by you? Will they treat you fairly? Or are some of them distant relatives or heirs, who might be inclined to second-guess you? Are they litigious? If that's the case, you may not want to have the responsibility of acting as trustee.

In any case, being trustee is a substantial responsibility. Please be careful to make sure it's a task you're willing to take on, and be sure to assemble a solid legal and accounting team, or use a corporate trustee or co-trustee, for backup and peace of mind.

CHAPTER 12:

Flexible Planning and the Whims of Congress

Chapter Contents: Changes in Assets, Changes in Laws ▶ Planning in an Uncertain World ▶ Portability and Some Simple But Effective Suggestions

> "Money isn't everything, but it sure keeps
> you in touch with your children."
> Attributed to J. Paul Getty

Changes in Assets, Changes in Laws. One of the reasons for the length of trust documents is that attorneys write them with the knowledge that the future will bring changes. Personal changes happen to the number and type of assets you have and to the number and type of beneficiaries. Changes in the form of revisions to the tax law are also coming. To cope with all of these uncertainties, trusts need flexibility. As shown by the table below, the tax environment has been in flux for many years.

In Figure 12-1 is the federal estate tax exemption schedule for the period beginning before the 1990's, up to the year 2011, as mandated by EGTRRA:

EGTRRA Exemptions and Tax Rates

Years	Exemption	Maximum Tax Rate
Pre-2000's	$600,000	55%
2000/01	$675,000	50%
2002/03	$1,000,000	49%
2004/05	$1,500,000	47%
2006	$2,000,000	46%
2007/08	$2,000,000	45%
2009	$3,500,000	45%
2010	Unlimited	0
2011	$1,000,000	55%

Figure 12-1

The President and Congress always have four theoretically possible choices when they evaluate existing tax laws: (1) no change, (2) higher taxes, (3) lower taxes, or (4) no tax. President Obama has indicated that the changes scheduled for 2010 and thereafter will not occur, and the 2009 tax rate and exemption levels will be continued into the future. In this case, the 2009 levels of exemption will roll forward, and the exemption will remain at $3,500,000. No substantial adjustment to the tax rate has been scheduled to occur.

Because of political reasons, the least likely possibility from 2009's perspective would have been eliminating estate taxes completely. Among elected officials, it has always been desirable to be able to tell the voting public they've lowered the burden on most of the taxpayers, but didn't let the very rich off the hook. Of course, very rich is a relative concept: a $500,000 residence in rural West Virginia is probably palatial, while in suburban parts of California, $500,000 may only buy a two bedroom fixer-upper. Nevertheless, with a huge federal budget to support, it is highly unlikely the estate tax would be eliminated or even scaled back significantly.

Even before the President's announcement, I felt strongly for the past few years that Congress and the President would make changes in 2009, and the scheduled changes in exemptions for 2010 and 2011 wouldn't occur as EGTRRA required. It didn't seem likely that Congress would let the estate tax exemption expire one year, then come back at the 10-year old level the following year. But because Congress has had such a very hard time agreeing about these issues, there's been no solid consensus behind the changes. Instead, I think Congress and the President have mentally labeled the President's proposed changes as interim measures that can be reexamined after some time has passed. For the taxpayer, the effect will be to keep the estate tax system in place, but still in flux, for the next few years.

In the future, I expect the capital gains tax rate to change, but there's no telling when or how often changes will occur. The President and Congress may try to balance the budget by increasing the long terms capital gains tax rate from the 2009 level of 15%, but I believe it will remain lower than income tax or estate tax rates.

It is likely that there will be a change in the method used for calculating the basis of appreciated property transferred as a result of a taxpayer's death. In the past, there's been a step-up in basis for property that is inherited, so the property gets a basis equal to the market value at the date of death. In essence, the heirs are treated as though they bought the property at that time, and when they later sell the property, they pay taxes only on gain that occurs after they own it. Most other capital gains avoidance mechanisms, like the 1031 Exchange explained in Chapter 15, just defer tax, which the taxpayer must pay later. This is one of the few cases of true tax forgiveness. Of course, you have to die to take advantage of it. The President and Congress will probably try to limit how much property qualifies to be stepped up. If some of your property doesn't get a step-up, you take the basis the original owner had. Without a step-up when you sell the property, you'll report and pay tax on all the gains made since the original owner bought it. Planning vehicles that transfer the property while you're alive, rather than at death, will be more attractive if the step-up in basis is removed.

Planning in an Uncertain World. But what if we make plans based on an incorrect assumption about future tax law changes? After all, the President and Congress have such difficulty reaching consensus that the system may well change again. Flexibility in planning will minimize financial and tax risk, no matter how the changes roll out. To prove it, let's try looking at the future and varying the assumptions about what Congress will do.

First, if you died before EGTRRA, your estate paid taxes according to the old estate tax rates and exemption. That's the first line of Table 12-1 at the beginning of this Chapter. If you died after EGTRRA but before any new tax law changes, your estate will pay estate tax and have the exemption according to the schedule for the year of death.

Let's move forward in time. As EGTRRA was originally written, if the President and Congress took no action, then there would be no estate tax at all in 2010. That's what it means to have an unlimited exemption.

If you die in 2010, and there's no change in the law, you'd pay the same amount of estate tax whether you have a Living Trust or not, namely zero. The basic tax saving aspect of any estate plan isn't needed, because there's no estate tax to avoid.

Don't assume you'd have wanted to revoke your trust at the start of 2010, though. There are several good reasons why you shouldn't. First, without a trust, you'd pay the maximum in probate fees. With a trust, you'd save probate fees entirely. Second, roll the clock forward to 2011 and assume you're still alive. Let's also make the assumption that the President and Congress were unable to change the EGTRRA schedule of estate tax laws. Under EGTRRA, the estate tax would return in 2011 with only $1,000,000 of exemption and a maximum estate tax rate of 55%.

Under the current plan to extend the 2009 tax levels and exemptions into the future, potential estate tax liability lurks for everyone whose estate might exceed $3,500,000 in value. A properly implemented Living Trust will help the married couple shelter $7,000,000 from estate taxes, rather than $3,500,000, so there's a dramatic benefit from planning as the tax laws now look.

Portability and Some Simple But Effective Suggestions. There's another possible change under proposed new estate tax legislation. Some of the proposals to fix the estate tax laws would make the exemptions in federal law portable. If portability of exemptions passes, it will make the use of the exemption of each of the spouses available to all estates, whether or not they use a trust. The mechanics of this aren't completely settled, but would likely take shape as follows: If a spouse dies, the community property rule permits passage of all of that spouse's assets to the other spouse without estate tax. At the death of the second spouse, any exemption the first spouse had that wasn't used would be added to the exemption available to the second spouse. If there was no lifetime gifting, the second spouse will get to apply up to double their own exemption at the time of their death. To simplify, look at the following schedule under EGTRRA. If the law provided for automatic portability, all married couples would get to skip to the third column of the Figure 12-2, whether or not they had a trust in place.

EGTRRA With Trust-Based or Portable Exemptions

Years	Exemption	Exemption for Married Couple with Trust, or Married Couple with Portable Exemptions
Pre-2000's	$600,000	$1,200,000
2000/01	$675,000	$1,350,000
2002/03	$1,000,000	$2,000,000
2004/05	$1,500,000	$3,000,000
2006	$2,000,000	$4,000,000
2007/08	$2,000,000	$4,000,000
2009	$3,500,000	$7,000,000
2010 (proposed)	$3,500,000	$7,000,000
2011 (proposed)	$3,500,000	$7,000,000

Figure 12-2

If portability passes, many commentators will doubtless state that existing trust documents must immediately be rewritten. They'll argue that the new law does away with the need to create a Bypass Trust.

I'll be much more cautious about changing my trust for at least three reasons.

First, there's no guarantee Congress won't change the tax law again and revive the need for the Bypass Trust. Suppose you create a new, simplified trust because Bypass Trusts aren't needed. When the first spouse dies, no Bypass Trust is set up. Years pass before the second spouse dies, and during that time, the law gets rewritten so that Bypass Trusts are needed again. It may be impossible to create one retroactively. Remember, it's at the death of the second spouse that the taxes kick in. That could be troublesome if the Bypass Trust gets eliminated from a plan because of taxpayer optimism.

If Congress does act to make the exemption portable, you should look at your plan and at your assets and liabilities. Simplify your trust, but only if you are confident that your estate will contain less money than will be taxable now and throughout the foreseeable future. If this fits your situation, you can amend your trust to eliminate references to the Sub-Trusts, and insert a new section directing that the trust be managed as a single pot trust, without need for the creation of Bypass, Survivor, or QTIP Trusts.

On the other hand, if your estate could be subject to tax, then try to get the best of both worlds. An amendment can be created which acknowledges possible future changes in the laws affecting trusts. Your amendment could provide that at the first death, your spouse gets to decide whether or not to create Sub-Trusts as set forth in the original trust. The choice should be based on the spouse's discretion. Your amendment will state that you wish to avoid estate tax if possible, but you do not want to subject your spouse to unnecessary management burdens. If the level of your assets, and the tax laws in effect at the time of your death, indicate that creation of a Survivor's, Bypass, and QTIP Trust would save taxes, then the spouse may create and fund the Bypass Trust. If not, at the discretion of the surviving spouse, as trustee, the trust can be managed as a single pot trust.

Frankly, I'm keeping my trust as is. Because of the potential lag between the first and second death, it seems likely that even if portability is adopted, subsequent future changes in the tax law will revive the need for the Bypass Trust structure.

Second, I'm keeping my trust as part of my plan to avoid probate even if the tax law changes drastically. For example, if you live in Georgia, where probate is very simple and swift, the need for an estate planning trust is much less pressing. A will may do everything that you need. I live in California, and I want my family to avoid the expense and delays of the probate system. Even if estate taxes are abolished completely, I'll keep my trust. It's the only safe way to avoid probate.

Third, despite new changes to the tax laws, you may want to keep your Sub-Trust structure intact to protect your family. There's an extra degree of protection for your heirs, particularly your children, created by the Survivor/Bypass/QTIP Sub-Trust structure. This reason applies even if the changes to the law include portability, and/or the exemption amounts are so high, and the tax rate so low, that there's no tax saving from a trust.

In Chapter 9, I explained that in most trusts the Bypass and QTIP Trusts become irrevocable after the first death. Using the Bypass and QTIP Trust mechanism, the first spouse to die knows that the first spouse's share of the property will only go to the first spouse's children or heirs upon the death of the second spouse, and that a new partner of a surviving spouse can't pressure that spouse to change this. If this is a concern to you, it may be protection you want to keep, despite changes to the estate tax law.

PART II: AVOIDING TAXES AND SAFEGUARDING WEALTH

"Fraud and falsehood only dread examination. Truth invites it."
Samuel Johnson (1709–1784)

In this next section, I will explain and demonstrate strategies and tools that are used in planning for higher net worth estates. There are numerous strategies and plans that seem like they have nothing in common with each other, except perhaps weird rhyming acronyms like CRAT and GRAT. Take heart, there are actually some common threads between many of these advanced techniques. These similarities can help you understand and compare the different advanced ideas based on what they can accomplish and what legal structures and mathematical principles make them work.

In the next four Chapters, I will explain the tools that are available for each potential strategy, explore additional applications or uses for these tools, and explain some additional complications as well. By understanding the wealth management and asset planning options available and the principles upon which they work, you'll be better able to refine and personalize your planning. Keep in mind, your decisions about whether or not to use these strategies should include consideration about how these strategies fit your values and lifestyle.

CHAPTER 13:

GRATs and QPRTs

Chapter Contents: Estate Freeze Technique
▸ Actual Growth and Assumed Growth ▸ The
QPRT

"If the only tool you know how to use is a hammer, it's simple. Every problem in life looks like a nail. A hammer just isn't a very good tool if you're washing the windows."
Dave Spence, Tax Attorney

Estate Freeze Technique. The Estate Freeze describes several strategies for limiting estate tax liability by limiting the size of the estate. The purpose of these strategies is to ensure that growth of the asset isn't part of the parent's taxable estate when they die. These techniques work by moving assets out of a parent's estate, while the parents are living, and into the taxable estates of the next generation. The future growth associated with the assets is transferred to the next generation, freezing the size of the parents' taxable estate at a lower value.

Suppose, for example, a couple has stock in a startup company that may increase in value very dramatically. If they own that stock when they die, there will be a large estate tax liability. To avoid this liability, they transfer the asset to their children in a controlled and tax effective manner, by placing all or part of the startup company's stock into a special trust with their children as beneficiaries.

The Grantor Retained Annuity Trust, or GRAT, is a trust that creates such a beneficial estate freeze. Intentionally Defective Grantor Trusts (explained in Chapter 14), Family Limited Partnerships (explained in Chapter 14) and Charitable Lead Trusts (explained in Chapter 16) can all be used in a similar manner to help avoid estate taxes. I'll explain how the Estate Freeze works using the GRAT as my example.

Actual Growth and Assumed Growth. The GRAT estate tax avoidance strategy uses the mathematical difference between the actual rate at which investments in a trust grow and the Federal 7520 interest rate. The difference between the actual growth and the Federal 7520 interest rate is accumulated and passed to the heirs, avoiding estate or gift tax on those sums.

The Federal 7520 interest rate is the interest rate approved for certain transactions. For example, this is the rate the IRS uses to test whether the interest rate charged on a loan between family members is equitable. If the rate charged is less than the 7520 rate, then part of the loan is considered a gift. Published by the IRS monthly, the rate has fluctuated between about 3 and about 8 percent over the last five years, and its level affects this type of structure greatly. The rate published by the IRS in the month the GRAT is created is used throughout the life of the GRAT.

Suppose you put $1,000,000 in a trust and under the terms of the trust, it pays you an annuity with an annual payment. For this example, let's make it easy by assuming it's a two year trust. At the end of the second year, $1,000,000 will have been repaid to you, along with interest. Assume the 7520 interest rate when the trust was created was 3.4%. The trust will therefore pay you $1,068,000, split into two installments.

You put up $1,000,000, and the trust is obligated to repay you that amount, along with the statutorily required amount of interest. In fact, when the trust pays you $1,068,000 from a tax law perspective there's no net transfer of funds at all. You put the money in one of your pockets, then transferred it to another with some interest. See Figure 13-1.

GRAT Flow of Funds

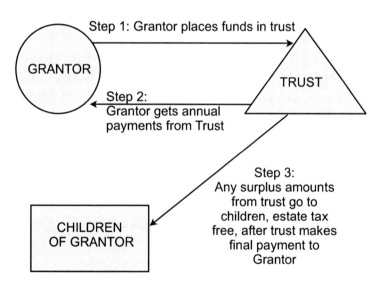

Figure 13-1

The interest that the trust pays out, however, is not mathematically related to what the investments in the trust will actually earn during those two years. That's where the tax-saving opportunity exists. Suppose the investments within the GRAT earned more than 3.4%. There will be enough money to pay you $1,068,000, with money left over in the trust.

The balance remaining in the trust can be payable to your heirs or children. For tax law purposes, when the GRAT is created, your children are getting a gift of the legal right to any remainder. How much is the gift worth? According to the IRS, on the day this GRAT is created, the gift is worth zero. If the trust assets earn exactly the interest rate the trust is obligated to repay to you, which is what the tax law expects, there'll be nothing left in the trust to distribute to the remainder beneficiaries. Since there is no financial gift to the beneficiaries, there's no gift tax.

Let's continue with our example. Assume your trust earned a net 10% on the invested trust money, so it generated $200,000 in income. With the original $1,000,000, the trust now has assets valued at $1,200,000. After paying you $1,068,000, there's $132,000 remaining in the trust. According to the gift and estate tax rules and the Federal 7520 rate, if the trust had earned exactly 3.4%, after paying you $1,068,000 there would be nothing left over. Once you're paid that amount in our example, however, there's $132,000 remaining in the trust. That remainder goes to your children without gift or estate tax. This remaining balance needn't be paid to them right at the end of year two; the funds may be controlled, invested, and continue to grow inside the trust and be distributed years later. Your children get safety and the benefit of this growth as well, all outside your taxable estate.

If the investments inside the GRAT don't earn enough to create a remainder or surplus, then there's no adverse gift or estate tax consequence. There's no benefit, either. The trust simply doesn't have any money left over to transfer to remainder beneficiaries once the payments to you have been made. No gain, but no pain.

The example I've given is very simple, and in reality, the math can be much more complex. You can vary the number of years, the type and timing of payments, and whether the GRAT is designed to distribute all of it's remainder assets gift tax free (called a zero out GRAT) or not. The outcome of the strategy, however, is that you have transferred money to a trust that repays you principal and pays a set interest rate. If the assets in the trust earn more than the interest rate set for the trust by the IRS, there's going to be a remainder left in the trust that passes to your beneficiaries without estate tax or gift tax burden.

The QPRT. The QPRT, or Qualified Personal Residence Trust is a favorite strategy of mine. The QPRT allows the trustor to transfer his or her residence to his or her heirs, on a predetermined schedule, while the trustor is still alive. For many clients, the family home has gradually increased in value over time and, in all likelihood, will continue to do so. If done correctly, the QPRT avoids substantial amounts of estate tax at the trustor's death.

To do this, an irrevocable trust is created, much like the format of an insurance trust, that holds title to the residence and transfers it over a period of years. The schedule for transferring the ownership over the years is based on actuarial tables in the Internal Revenue regulations. If the trustors die before the period is up, there's no penalty, but no partial victory, either. That is, if the trustors die before the QPRT is complete, the residence remains in the parents' estate, and is subject to estate tax.

QPRTs are interesting because many clients ask about them, but few actually implement one. People generally begin discussing a QPRT with enthusiasm about the potential tax break, but when they realize that their house will belong to their heirs at the end of the trust period, they get nervous. At some point, the questions start: "My kids won't really own my house. I mean, they couldn't make me pay rent. Right? There's a secret escape hatch?"

Nope. There's no secret escape hatch. At the end of the period, the beneficiaries of the trust really, legally, physically, and in every other way, own the parents' house. They can and should make the parents pay rent. But giving up the family home to this kind of trust doesn't feel right or safe to most people. This strategy involves a loss of control, which makes most folks unhappy, and that's often the end of the conversation.

If clients don't mind the loss of control, this is a very good tax shelter. Once the heirs own the home of the wealthy parents, having the parents paying rent actually helps reduce the size of the parent's taxable estate even further. Sometimes, clients use a QPRT for the transfer of a second house or vacation home. It can work well in this instance, especially if it's a house in a special location that you'd like your family to keep after you're gone.

It's also possible to intentionally set up a QPRT that only transfers a portion of the home to the beneficiaries. Another option is to do a series of GRATs or QPRTs, which planners refer to as laddered. Each trust transfers part of a property or investment. For example, rather than transferring the entire property in a single QPRT over 9 years, you create 3 QPRTs that transfer the property at phased intervals, say 1/3 at years 3, 6, and 9. Suppose the donor dies before year 9, say at year 7. A single 9 year QPRT would give no benefits and simply be ignored for tax purposes. In the case of the laddered QPRT, death at year 7, there would have been a transfer of 2/3 of the property from the first two completed transactions at years 3 and 6, and the third set for year 9 would be disregarded, so there's some benefit from a tax perspective.

CHAPTER 14:

The Family Limited Partnership

Chapter Contents: The Family Limited Partnership ("FLP") ▶ The FLP in Operation ▶ Valuation Discounts ▶ Intentionally Defective Trusts

In *The Adventures of Huckleberry Finn*, Mark Twain had these observations on the way family members can work out their differences:

> "Did you want to kill him, Buck?...What did he do to you?"
>
> "Him? He never done nothing to me."
>
> "Well, then, what did you want to kill him for?"
>
> "Why, nothing – only it's on account of the feud."
>
> "What's a feud? ..."
>
> "Well," says Buck, "a feud is this way: A man has a quarrel with another man, and kills him; then that other man's brother kills him; then the other brothers, on both sides, goes for one another; then the cousins chip in – and by and by everybody's killed off, and there ain't no more feud. But it's kind of slow, and takes a long time."
>
> "Has this one been going on long, Buck?"
>
> "Well, I should reckon! It started thirty year ago, or som'ers

along there. There was trouble 'bout something, and then a lawsuit to settle it; and the suit went agin one of the men, and so he up and shot the man that won the suit – which he would naturally do, of course. Anybody would."

Today, there are more peaceful options for working out family disagreements.

The Family Limited Partnership ("FLP"). The Family Limited Partnership is a management tool with a built-in estate tax advantage, namely, discounting. By fractionalizing or dividing the ownership of a business or entity, the Family Limited Partnership ("FLP") can have very beneficial effects on the valuation and taxation of the component parts of that entity. FLPs are also effective in creating an estate freeze, a concept introduced in the last chapter, which can also be very beneficial.

The Family Limited Partnership can be very useful, particularly in ongoing family businesses or family farms where the younger generation is getting involved in management. Suppose the family business has thrived, and the parents wish to pass some of the value and future growth to their children in a way that has tax advantages. They also wish to involve the younger generation in management, but they aren't ready to lose control of the business.

The FLP In Operation. FLPs are a specific type of limited partnership, and like all limited partnerships, they have two types of members: general partners and limited partners. The parents are usually the general partners, and as general partners they retain all of the management and control rights of the partnership. In a Family Limited Partnership, the general partners retain only a very small equity interest. The parents and children are usually all limited partners, and the limited partners own the majority of the equity. Limited partners don't have voting or management rights equal to their ownership share. In other words, parents can keep business control as general partners, while sharing and transferring the equity or wealth to themselves and their children to hold as limited partners. See Figure 14-1. (For more information about general and limited partnerships, please see Chapters 18 and 19.)

Family Limited Partnership Flow of Funds

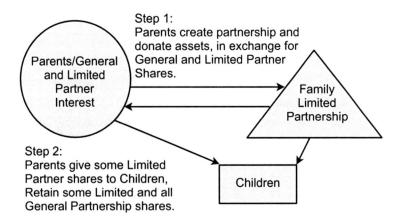

Step 1:
Parents create partnership and donate assets, in exchange for General and Limited Partner Shares.

Parents/General and Limited Partner Interest

Family Limited Partnership

Step 2:
Parents give some Limited Partner shares to Children, Retain some Limited and all General Partnership shares.

Children

- Parents retain control through General Partner shares;
- Parents retain part of growth by keeping some Limited Partner shares;
- Limited Partner Shares sold or given to children have discounted value for tax purposes.

Figure 14-1

The order of the initial steps depends on the nature of the assets being transferred, and sometimes on the local property tax laws. Some states, such as California, have a property tax system which requires reassessment, and may require additional property taxes whenever real estate is transferred. As I explained in Chapter 9, there is an exception to this rule for living trusts, so your deed from yourself individually to yourself as trustee doesn't cause reassessment or additional tax. There is a similar exception for FLPs.

In order to qualify for this exception, the real estate must be transferred from individual owners to a partnership or other entity, and that entity must be owned by the original property owners. The owners must hold the same ownership proportions through the partnership or other new entity that they held before the transfer. Where this is the case, there is no reassessment, and no additional taxes due when the property is transferred. For example, if Mom and Pop were co-owners, 50/50, of a farm, and they transferred it to the newly created Mom & Pop Partnership, of which they were 50/50 owners, there would be no reassessment and no additional property taxes. To take advantage of this exemption, the parents create a Family Limited Partnership and are the only partners when they first transfer the property. Later they will give or sell the children limited partnership shares.

If real estate property tax reassessment isn't an issue, the Family Limited Partnership is usually formed with minimal assets. At the same time the FLP is formed, the parents also transfer money to their children, usually only a nominal amount. The children use this money to buy limited partnership shares. The parents then sell the family business or other major asset to the FLP, in exchange for limited partnership shares for themselves. Since the parents also retained all of the general partnership interest, they continue to manage the assets or business.

The parents often continue to make transfers of limited partnership interests, either by gift or sale, to the children. Many parents make this transfer annually and take advantage of the annual tax-free gifting amounts, currently $13,000 per child from each parent (explained in Chapter 4). The parents own the general partnership interests and manage all of the partnership assets, for which they receive a management fee.

Distributions of earnings or profits from the partnership are made in accordance with various partners' percentage of equity in the limited partnership shares.

The Family Limited Partnership has a number of advantages:

- Parents can transfer wealth to their beneficiaries without reducing the transferees' productivity and initiative, which might result had the parents transferred cash instead of a share in an ongoing business;

- The FLP's valuation discounts for determining the value of partnership interests reduce estate tax liability;

- The FLP can include a right of first refusal. Before family partners dispose of their holdings to an outside person, they can require that the share be offered for sale to family members;

- The FLP provides some (limited) protection against creditors; it can protect assets of the junior members in a divorce proceeding to some extent.

The most powerful aspect of the FLP is the potential estate tax saving through the use of valuation discounts.

Valuation Discounts. Valuation principles are an important part of this strategy. Impressive tax advantages come with the creation of the FLP, because of discounts for lack of control and lack of marketability. Value, as defined by courts, appraisers, and taxing entities, is dependent on market prices.

There are three methods, generally, for arriving at an appraised value, and these are (1) the replacement costs method, (2) the income method, and (3) the comparable sales method.

The replacement costs method values the property based on what it would cost to rebuild or replace the property. It works well for recently built items, such as new homes or commercial buildings. Standardized figures on the construction cost per square foot for buildings or homes are available from various industry sources, so it is possible to compute what it would cost to rebuild the structure being evaluated. When the structure is older, this becomes a less reliable method. Are you going to rebuild a 1960's building with 1960's technology, or as it would be built today? For economists, this problem, sometimes called the index number problem, is extremely thorny. With building code changes and improved building methods, is a home built in the 1940's equivalent to current construction? These fundamental differences can make certain kinds of comparison meaningless, especially over long periods of time, like comparing a jet plane to a horse-drawn cart.

The income method works well for commercial buildings or income (rental) property. To determine market value by the income method, we compare what similar properties earn in rental income, and then compare market sales of those properties in the area. The relationship between sales price and the rental income can be expressed as a ratio, called the capitalization ratio or cap rate. By using the income generated from the subject property, the cap rate can then be used to determine the value of the property in question. Of course, if the property generates no income, this method can't be applied.

The comparable sales method involves finding sales of similar properties, and computing a value based upon those sales. It is probably the most direct and reliable method if the market is stable and the building is not unique.

Chapter Fourteen: The Family Limited Partnership

There is both fact and interpretation involved in all valuation computations. The facts are data about sales or rentals and the interpretation lies in determining how the properties compare and adjusting appropriately for differences. Valuation specialists, such as appraisers or economists, may use all three methods if possible, or only one or two depending on circumstances.

The following discussion is about shares of stock, but the same principles apply to ownership shares of any small business, whether it's a partnership, limited partnership or corporation.

At any given time, one share of a large corporation's publicly traded stock is worth the same to everybody. Assume these shares are freely traded on a national market, and the control of the company is vested in thousands of shareholders. Your shares are no different than anyone else's, and if the stock is listed at $10 per share on a national stock exchange, it's going to be worth $10 in the market and $10 to the tax authorities.

On the other hand, being a 10% shareholder or limited partner of somebody else's family business isn't worth the same thing to different people. Someone in the family, who's well tied in with the controlling owners, might see this fractional interest as being worth 10% of the underlying value of the business. To someone outside the family, it's worth something less than that. An outsider has little control, because they may have little influence over the family members. Also, this 10% share has limited marketability. Few buyers would be eager to buy this shareholder's position and become the next outsider in this family business. The 10% share of the family business isn't worthless, but it's not worth the full face value because of this lack of control and lack of marketability.

Example: In the context of the limited partnership, suppose the family creates a Family Limited Partnership with $1 million in assets. The parent decides to give a child a 1% limited partnership interest. Intuitively, it seems that the 1% interest is worth $10,000, because that is the pro-rata value of the underlying assets. However, because of the lack of marketability and lack of control associated with the limited partnership interest, a willing buyer might pay a willing seller only $7,000 for that interest. This is a 30% discount on the value of the underlying asset. Suppose a parent gave a child 1/3 of $1,000,000. The taxing authorities recognize this as a gift of $333,000. However, by using a FLP, the senior generation may transfer partnership interests representing 1/3 of the partnership at a 30% discount. Instead of valuing the partnership share at $333,000, the partnership share is worth $234,000. Since there is a limit to the amount that can be transferred to a child without paying gift taxes, being able to discount the value of a transfer is quite powerful. The gift may be rolled out over a number of years rather than all at once if the parents prefer.

The IRS may, of course, dispute or disallow discounts taken on an estate or gift tax return. In an audit, the question is usually about the valuation discount, or about the form and business purpose of the partnership entity itself. In the litigation stage, taxpayers usually win these suits if the transaction was executed and structured correctly. Because of this, it's very important to hire a qualified valuation expert even in the planning stages. Before any transfer of a partnership interest, it is very important to determine the value of the interest, taking into account all appropriate discounts.

For FLP's, the amount of the discount varies depending on facts and circumstances relevant to each asset and to each partnership. The available discount under the case law can be as high as 30 or 40%. However, I am conservative and seldom rest easy with a recommendation that goes higher than the low 30's. Taxpayers typically win cases when the FLP was established and administered properly and had a real management function. The IRS wins in cases where the partnership structure is not respected, or followed, by the partners. It is particularly damaging when there is no reason other than tax avoidance for creating the partnership, and where the parties got aggressive and claimed overly large valuation discounts.

When the FLP process is first laid out, the actual numbers that will be generated are impossible to gauge with certainty. Certain information doesn't exist until the process is actually underway. At the outset we don't know how long the parents will actually live. Nor do we know for certain what the estate tax law will be like in the future. We don't know whether the assets or the investments will provide the return we expected, or some higher or lower rate of return. Also, some parents give shares in the FLP to their children over time, rather than all at once. These, and many other factors, influence the performance of the FLP as it rolls out.

The beneficiaries of a FLP get an asset transferred to them at a discounted rate, and growth in that asset will occur outside the parents' estate as well. This type of strategy is an estate freeze, like the GRAT discussed in Chapter 13.

Intentionally Defective Trusts. Similarly, intentionally defective trusts can be used for estate freeze transactions. Intentionally Defective Grantor Trusts, sometimes referred to as a IDGT, IDIT or DGIT, are defective in a very technical sense.

The Intentionally Defective Trust strategy makes use of the basic fact that the rules for estate tax and the rules for income tax are not identical. The Intentionally Defective Trust moves an asset to another person's estate, such as the grantor's children, for estate tax purposes. Like Family Limited Partnership shares, in a successful Intentionally Defective Trust, growth of the assets for estate tax purposes occurs in the children's estate, not in the parent's taxable estate. The trust can be effective in the estate tax world, but defective under the income tax laws, by use of an intentionally inserted defect. Being defective in this sense is not an accident, and will not lead to fines, penalties, or misapplication of taxable amounts. Rather, the defect means that because certain powers were reserved to the trust creator, the trust won't be regarded as a separate taxpayer for income tax purposes. This way, the grantor or trustor continues to pay any income tax on earnings from the trust, but for estate tax purposes, the heirs are the ones experiencing future gain on the asset.

There are additional refinements which can maximize the benefit of the Intentionally Defective Trust strategy. The Grantor can sell the assets to the Trust, and, rather than take cash, take back a promissory note. If the Trust uses Self Canceling Installment Notes, or SCINs, to make the payments, it can create additional benefits at the Grantor's death. SCINs are a special type of promissory note which get cancelled or forgiven to the extent they are still outstanding at the grantor's death. This can substantially enhance the estate tax benefit by reducing the size of the grantor's estate.

CHAPTER 15:

1031 Exchanges and Strategies for Liquidity Events

Chapter Contents: Liquidity Events and Capital Gains ▶ *The 1031 Exchange* ▶ *1031 Issues*

"With great power comes great responsibility."
Attributed to Spiderman's Uncle Ben

"With great infusions of wealth come great potential tax liabilities."
Attributed to Warren Buffett

Many clients have questions about the best way to deal with assets that have increased dramatically in value. The Family Limited Partnership (Chapter 14), the Charitable Trust (Chapter 16), and the 1031 Exchange all have potential uses in this context. It's important to understand each of the strategies individually so that you understand how they compare.

These strategies come into play when a sudden transition or event in your life results in a significant increase in your wealth. Such a transition or event could be the sale of the family business, a real estate investment, or a stock option from a successful company. These liquidity events bring challenges, and the tax and financial impacts need to be evaluated in the context of your overall plan.

Liquidity Events and Capital Gains. Suppose you have a rental home that has increased in value over the years. You'd like to sell it and buy another rental property. It may be that you want to trade up to a larger property, for example, to a duplex or a small apartment building; or it may be that you've taken most of the depreciation out of the property so that there's no income tax advantage to continuing to own this property. There are many reasons that may motivate you to sell your property and buy another. The downside to selling the property is that you will have to pay capital gains tax on any gains when the property is sold. Wouldn't it be great if you could structure the deal so you could sell one property, then purchase another, and postpone payment of any capital gains taxes?

The 1031 Exchange. It's possible to postpone the capital gains tax impact of a sale of an investment asset through a 1031 Exchange, sometimes called a Starker Exchange or a Like Kind Exchange. For simplicity, I'll use the name 1031 Exchange, which is a reference to Internal Revenue Code Section 1031. This section establishes a set of rules under which a taxpayer can sell and then repurchase similar kinds of investments and defer payment of taxes on any gains. Instead of a simple sale, payment of the capital gains tax, then purchase of a new asset, the taxpayer rolls from one asset into a new asset in a tax free exchange. While other types of investment assets qualify for this treatment, the 1031 is mainly used in real estate transactions.

I'll use a two-part hypothetical real estate transaction to help you understand the power and the limitations of the 1031 strategy. I'll demonstrate the simplest case, where a taxpayer sells one rental property and buys another with no attempt to control tax liability. At the same time, I'll demonstrate a 1031 Exchange strategy using the same facts.

I'll make a few simplifying assumptions throughout these examples. Most income-producing assets experience wear and tear over time, and eventually need to be repaired or replaced. The Internal Revenue Code permits a taxpayer to take deductions against the income from such an asset to reflect the asset's limited lifespan. If a taxpayer owns a rental house, for example, that taxpayer typically takes depreciation deductions against the rental income. The taxpayer benefits while he owns the rental house because he pays less income tax, due to the depreciation deductions; however, as a matter of tax accounting, the depreciation deductions reduce the taxpayer's basis in the property.

Eventually, when the property is sold, this must be accounted for. The taxable gain on a sale is the difference between the sales price and the basis, and where depreciation has been taken, the lowered basis effectively increases the gain. This is recognized in the tax accounting when the property is sold, and the increased gain means an increase in taxes due after the sale. Accountants call this recapture of depreciation, and it must be factored into the tax accounting for investment property.

For mathematical simplicity in these examples I'll ignore depreciation recapture. I'll also ignore brokerage fees or other transactional costs, and I'll round off the numbers in the calculations. Also, for the purpose of calculating state taxes, my examples assume a taxpayer lives in California; please remember, though, that state tax laws are not uniform and you need to ascertain the effect of the applicable state law on your particular transaction.

Assume you bought a rental house, Property #1, for $100,000 many years ago, that is now worth $1,000,000, and you're considering selling it. Assume, also, that there's another rental house, Property #2, you could purchase for $1,000,000.

Examples: The first transaction I'll refer to is the sale of Property #1, the rental house you already own. First, I'll demonstrate the impact of selling it without tax planning, then as the first part of a 1031 Exchange.

Sale of Property #1 With No Tax Planning: If you sell the rental property for $1,000,000 and it had a $100,000 basis, your capital gains tax liability is calculated as follows:

Capital Gains	Fed Tax	CA Tax	Total Tax	Net Profit	Available for Re-Investment
$900,000	15%	9.3%	$219,000	$681,000	$781,000

You get $681,000 of net profit, plus the original $100,000 you invested, and the government gets the rest. You've kept the transaction simple, but by ignoring the tax consequences, you have an immediate tax liability and must write checks to the taxing authorities totaling $219,000.

Alternative Sale of Property #1 as First Part of a 1031 Exchange: Now, I'll assume you are doing a 1031 Exchange. When you sell the first property I again assume your sale price is $1,000,000, and that you originally purchased the property for $100,000. As part of a 1031 exchange, this part of the transaction looks far different from the sale with no tax planning:

Capital Gains	Fed Tax	CA Tax	Basis	Available for Re-Investment
$900,000	Deferred	Deferred	$100,000	$1,000,000

Examples: The purchase of Property #2 is about another rental home which is listed for sale for a price of $1,000,000. I'll assume that you've sold Property #1, and you want to purchase Property #2. For these examples, I'll continue to make the same simplifying assumptions as above, namely that there's no depreciation recapture, no costs of sale, and I'll round off the calculations. I'm also going to assume that after you purchase Property #2, you own it for two years and then sell it for $1,100,000.

Purchase of Property #2 With No Tax Planning: If you paid the capital gains tax after the first transaction and reinvested your profits, you had $781,000 to put towards Property #2. The listed purchase price is $1,000,000, so you need another $219,000 to complete the purchase. I'll assume you used money from your savings to complete the purchase.

I assume that you sell Property #2 two years after buying it, for $1,100,000. The taxable gain, when you later sell the property, will be the difference between the sale price and the basis. For property #2 purchased without the 1031 exchange, your basis has two parts: the proceeds from Property #1 of $781,000, and your additional investment of $219,000, or a total of $1,000,000. The gain on the sale is the difference between the sale price you receive, $1,100,000 and your basis of $1,000,000, so the taxable gain is $100,000. This gain will be taxed at a combined federal and state rate of 24.3%.

Capital Gains	Fed Tax	CA Tax	Total Tax	Net Profit
$100,000	15%	9.3%	$24,000	$76,000

Summary: If you ignored the tax effects on both transactions, your combined profit on the two sales, after taxes, was $757,000. You received back your original investment of $100,000, and you paid $243,000 in taxes.

Purchase of Property #2 as Second Part of 1031 Exchange: As part of a 1031 Exchange, you invest the entire gross proceeds from the sale of Property #1, $1,000,000, when you purchase property #2. When you eventually sell Property #2 as part of the 1031 Exchange, the basis is the same basis you had when you sold Property #1, which was only $100,000. If you sell Property #2 for $1,100,000 two years later, the gains from both properties are taxed at the time of the second sale. In this example, that's 1,100,000 - 100,000 or $1,000,000 of taxable gain.

Capital Gains	Fed Tax	CA Tax	Total Tax	Net Profit
$1,000,000	15%	9.3%	$243,000	$757,000

Summary: The net profit and total taxes paid on the two transactions are identical after the second sale has closed in this example. That's why the 1031 Exchange is referred to as a tax deferral, rather than a tax forgiveness strategy, because it affects when the taxes are due more than how much is due.

Nonetheless, there are advantages to the 1031 Exchange. In the example where there was no tax planning, you only had $781,000 after paying the taxes on the first sale. An additional $219,000 was needed to close the purchase of Property #2. In the 1031 Exchange example, you had the full $1,000,000 available for purchase of Property #2, because the payment of taxes was postponed.

In actuality, my assumption that you could easily raise the money in the first example may not be accurate. I ignored any cost to raising the additional funds, or the possibility that additional funds might not be available.

In actual transactions, fund availability often creates a substantial difference to the gains realized from real estate transactions. The 1031 Exchange postpones the payment of capital gains taxes, giving the taxpayer more money to put towards the purchase of the new property. Suppose the additional funds aren't available, and you purchase your second property with the funds left over after the first purchase. Again, we'll ignore depreciation recapture and we'll round off our results. Assume, also, that investment real property is generally going up in price at 5% per year. If you did no tax planning, you had only $781,000 to invest. A $781,000 property appreciating at 5% per year, and sold after two years would return $859,000, a gross profit of $78,000. In the case of the 1031 exchange, you had $1,000,000 to invest, and at 5% appreciation per year and a sale at the end of year two, you could sell the property for $1,100,000 or a gross profit of $100,000. After paying taxes on the two transactions, the 1031 Exchange earned an extra $16,500 in two years. Over a longer timeframe, the effect becomes even more dramatic. And it sometimes happens that a more valuable property will appreciate faster than a lower priced property, leading to even higher overall profits in a 1031 Exchange transaction.

1031 Issues. There are highly technical rules in a 1031 Exchange. These rules include determining whether the property is similar enough to qualify for 1031 treatment, the tax treatment of the money that's put in or taken out of the transaction, and how the money is handled during the transaction. There are also very important rules about the timing of the sales and purchase of replacement property. If you get any of it wrong, there can be serious tax consequences.

Even with these restrictions, however, many people find that the 1031 Exchange is a good tool for them. If an investor is experienced at managing rental properties, he may want to use the 1031 Exchange strategy to sell one property and buy another. When he is ready to sell that property, he can enter into another 1031 Exchange and defer the taxes yet again.

Some investors, though, find themselves caught in a cycle of exchanges rather like a merry-go-round ride. They've done a series of 1031 Exchanges, but eventually, they want the merry-go-round to stop so they can stop doing exchanges. They may be ready to quit managing rental real estate and buy into a less risky or less demanding type of investment. They may want to invest in a different asset class altogether, or they may want to spend the money they've made. At that time, under the 1031 rules, they will have to pay all of the deferred capital gains tax.

A further potential refinement to the 1031 Exchange is for the new property purchased to be part of a REIT, in a strategy called an upREIT. A REIT, or Real Estate Investment Trust, is a company that buys a large number of properties and manages them in a trust owned in shares by many investors. The investor is no longer managing a single piece or group of properties personally, and may be able to sell small chunks or parts of the investment if needed. Another advantage is that the shares in the trust may become tradable on the stock exchanges like other large companies.

There are many steps to trading a property into a group property, turning it into a REIT, and eventually having the REIT going public. Be very cautious. This strategy is new and has not been tested by the courts. Moreover, with such a strategy, at the end of the day, the investor is still invested in real estate. If the goal is to diversify these funds into a different asset class or type altogether, this is not a very good fit.

CHAPTER 16:

The Charitable Trust

Chapter Contents: The Charitable Remainder Trust ▸ Hillary Clinton's Book Deal ▸ Types of Charitable Trusts ▸ Annuity Versus Unitrust Payment Options ▸ Comparison

"The manner of giving is worth more than the gift."
Pierre Corneille (1606–1684)

The Charitable Trust is a powerful tax saving strategy. There are several types of Charitable Trusts, with different benefits. One of the most potent benefits, however, is that assets can be bought and sold inside of the trust without capital gains tax. Charitable trusts can convert assets from appreciated but low-yield or riskier holdings to higher yield or safer investments while avoiding or postponing taxes otherwise due on the sale of the assets. Here, the powerful concept behind the strategy is to keep more money working within the trust, thereby creating additional wealth and/or a more secure income stream from the assets.

Suppose that you and your spouse are retirement age. You own some rental real estate that has grown in value, and a developer is interested in buying it. You need steady income for the rest of your life, and you'd like to leave a legacy to your favorite charity as well. A charitable trust can create a structure that will provide you secure income during your life and make a charitable gift upon your death in the most tax efficient way. The CRT creates a very efficient tax savings structure by using charitable giving in conjunction with avoiding or deferring capital gains and/or avoiding estate tax liability.

The Charitable Remainder Trust. If you have an asset that has appreciated greatly in value, you may be a candidate to utilize a Charitable Remainder Trust. If you simply sold the asset to diversify your investments, you'd have to pay capital gains taxes. If you gave the asset directly to a charity, you'd get a deduction, but nothing else. During retirement, many of us need income from our appreciated assets for ourselves as well. A Charitable Remainder Trust allows you to transfer the property to a trust that will distribute it to a charity years in the future. This allows you to earn income from the property now and get a charitable tax deduction now. If the math is right, it's possible to get more from the Charitable Trust strategy than by selling the asset outright and paying the tax. And at the end of the trust's existence, the charity gets a substantial gift. See Figure 16-1.

Hillary Clinton's Book Deal. The *New York Times* ran an article years ago concerning Mrs. Clinton's book, *It Takes a Village: And Other Lessons Children Teach Us*. According to the *Times* (April 19, 1998), the Clintons received income from the book, paid tax on it, then donated two years sales proceeds to charity. They paid $291,756 in taxes, but they could have paid only $167,532 in taxes by having the royalties paid to a charitable trust. By using this strategy, the Clintons would have paid less in taxes and the charity would have gotten about 22% more than the $840,000 they received.

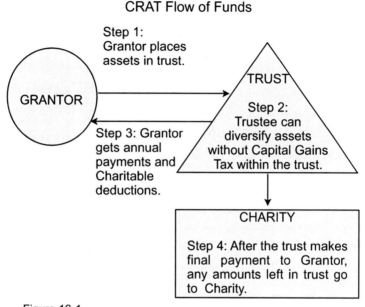

Figure 16-1

Types of Charitable Trusts. Charitable Trusts differ according to how and when payments are made. These are called Charitable Remainder Trusts (CRT) and Charitable Lead Trusts (CLT).

- A remainder trust gives property to the charity at the end of its term. During its term it pays income to a non-charitable beneficiary, typically the people who created the trust.

- A lead trust is just the opposite. The charity gets the income from the trust and the property returns to a non-charitable beneficiary, usually children or grandchildren, at the end of the trust period.

Either of these types of trusts can use different methods for making payments during their term.

- An annuity trust makes payments required by the terms of the trust at a fixed dollar amount per year. A Charitable Remainder Trust that pays on an annuity formula is called a Charitable Remainder Annuity Trust (CRAT) and a Charitable Lead Trust that pays on the annuity formula is a Charitable Lead Annuity Trust (CLAT).

- A unitrust makes payments as a percentage of the value of the trust investments, as appraised each year. A Charitable Remainder Trust that pays on a unitrust formula is called a Charitable Remainder Unitrust (CRUT) and a Charitable Lead Trust that pays on the unitrust formula is a Charitable Lead Unitrust (CLUT).

With respect to Unitrusts, there are still other possible variations, having to do with the ability to alter the payout amounts:

- Standard CRUTs pay a percentage value of the total assets each year.
- NICRUTs are are versions which only pay net income.
- NIMCRUTs allow makeup of the net income if asset growth is variable.
- FlipCRUTs are hybrids in which a trust can convert from a NICRUT or NIMCRUT to a standard CRUT.

The strategies behind the refinements usually have to do with the characteristics of the property in the trust. For example, when the property doesn't produce a steady income but has high value, one of these variations of the standard charitable trust is usually called for.

In addition to helping a charity, the charitable trust donor is generally trying to capture one of two kinds of benefits for himself. The donor is either avoiding or postponing capital gains tax on an appreciated asset, or avoiding estate tax when the property transfers to heirs. At the same time, the donor will get a charitable deduction on his income taxes in some actuarially determined amount, and the donor can make his portfolio more secure by buying and selling investments in the tax-efficient environment of the CRT.

Math plays a big part, but so does public spirit. The mathematical results can be altered by changing the method of payment or changing the calculation method. But in order to make the strategy work, at some point a charity must get a gift of some amount. Folks who are very charitably minded often set up a charitable trust which gives them little personal tax benefit. Others who are more interested in the tax benefits, structure the deal so there is relatively more benefit to themselves or their family than to the charity.

For folks who are charitably inclined but are concerned with the negative effect the eventual charitable gift will have on their family's wealth, the donor can take out a life insurance policy. At the end of the transaction, when the property goes to the charity, the donor's family gets wealth replacement through the insurance policy. In other words, the proceeds of the policy replace the value of whatever was given away.

There are complex rules that determine allowable amounts of return to the recipient and to the charity as required by the Internal Revenue Code and Regulations. Allowable payouts are based on the interest rate at the time of the creation of the trust, the length of time the trust lasts, the amount it will pay to the recipients, and other factors. And remember, because the available tax benefits exist to permit and encourage charitable giving, the payments can't just be set to any number the taxpayer chooses.

Here are a few examples of the strategy at work:

Example: Suppose you wanted to use a Charitable Remainder Trust in conjunction with the sale of a rental property that you bought for

$100,000, and are selling for $1,000,000. As in the Chapter 15, on the 1031 Exchange, we're assuming no depreciation or other issues to complicate the example, and calculations are being rounded off. If you sold the property outright and paid the gain, you'd net about $681,000 and the capital gains tax would be roughly $219,000.

Let's assume that as owner of the rental property you want to get some income for the rest of your life from the trust. Assume, also, that when you die, you want the remaining balance in the trust to go to a recognized charity. Based on the current Internal Revenue Code and Regulations, you could create a Charitable Remainder Annuity Trust that gives you a 5.15% payout of $46,350 per year for the rest of your life. If you owned the property with your spouse, you can have the payments continue for both of your lives rather than terminating when you die. Of course, this generally means the payments will be lower. Or, you can choose to get payments over a fixed term of years, up to 20 years. In this hypothetical case, the trust term could be set at 11 years, and pay as much as 9.8% per year, or $88,000 each year. The change happens because the trustor only gets paid through year 11, then the charity gets the balance. Shortening the trust term means the grantor can have a higher payout and still pass the tests from the regulations under the Internal Revenue Code.

In both cases, you get a charitable deduction. With the first example, the charitable deduction you'd get would be approximately $330,000. If you couldn't use all of the deduction in the first year, that deduction can be carried over for five years. The deduction for the charitable gift in the second case is also lower, only $91,000, because more of the money is going back to the grantor, faster. There's less money left for the charity and hence a lower deduction.

What if the investments made by the trust aren't very good, and there's less money left over at the end? Or suppose they're better than average, and there's more left over than you planned? Neither affects your income from a Charitable Remainder Annuity Trust. You get only the specified payments. The charity gets what's left, which could be more, or less, than you initially calculated.

The equations used to calculate the payment amounts and deductions are more complex than I am demonstrating in these examples. Annuity trusts must meet a 5% probability test. That means the charitable deduction won't be allowed if more than a 5% probability exists that the trust will be exhausted before it makes payment to the charity. There are restrictions requiring the value of the remainder that goes to the charity to be at least 10% of the market value of the property that was originally transferred. Moreover, no annual payouts can exceed 50% of the fair market value of the trust. These regulations change from time to time, and the applicable published interest rate can change each month. (The rate in use in the month you create your trust is the interest rate for your trust throughout its term; changes in the rate only apply to new trusts when they are formed.) Due to the complexity of the regulations and the calculations required, you should work with a tax planning professional to help you set up this type of trust.

Annuity Versus Unitrust Payment Options. What choices does a grantor have about the manner the payments are calculated? There are two types of possible payouts, mentioned earlier in this Chapter.

The annuity calculation pays the same amount each year. This is beneficial to those who'd like to know exactly what they're getting each year. It can, however, drain the trust if the assets aren't invested wisely enough. Because of the actuarial tables used by the IRS, the calculations are such that the payouts from an annuity trust are usually more favorable to older clients. Remember that annuity, in this context, refers to payments which are made in a preset amount. There is no requirement that the trust invest assets in an annuity type of investment vehicle.

The other way of computing payments is to use the unitrust calculation, which computes the value of the assets in the trust annually and then pays the grantor a percentage of the total asset value. Since there is no pre-set or guaranteed amount in terms of the dollar value of the annual payment amount, the grantor doesn't know in advance what the payment will be. It will vary over the years, depending on how well the investments inside the trust have performed. However, unitrust payments are unlikely to ever drain the trust completely. They can also give the trustor an upside, as far as additional income. If the investments within the trust are very successful, the trust assets will grow in value, and so will the payouts. There is, however, some extra expense to using the unitrust payout method because the trust assets need to be valued or appraised each year.

A grantor focused on maximizing his family's well being, and not on the charity, can use some of the income paid from the trust to buy a life insurance policy. However, there's no legal or mathematical requirement that the grantor replace the value of what's given to the charity. For example, a family can puchase a policy of sufficient value to replace whatever is being given away. Suppose a $900,000 second-to-die policy is put in place. When the second spouse dies and the charity receives the remainder, the heirs receive an insurance policy payout which replaces the property given to the charity. The insurance is held in an Irrevocable Life Insurance Trust (ILIT) explained in detail in Chapter 17. Usually, the insurance policy is equal in value to the funds originally placed in the charitable trust. For the very sophisticated, the payments made to the grantor during his lifetime also increase the family wealth; conceptually, this means that even less insurance is required to restore mathematical equality.

If you normally donate money to charities each year, you may want to consider a Charitable Lead Trust. This strategy gives income to a charity but returns the leftover principal to trust beneficiaries, and often avoids significant amounts of estate tax. Here, the math is a little different. The same principle that worked for our GRAT in Chapter 13, with a refinement, is at work in the Charitable Lead Trust. In the GRAT, the principal amount is put into a trust, and is paid back to the grantor over time at a statutorily approved rate of interest. This makes the transaction a zero from the grantor's point of view. If the investments in the trust outperformed the 7520 rate, the leftover amount is transferred to the grantor's heirs without gift or estate tax.

Just like the GRAT, the 7520 interest rate mechanism is at work in a Charitable Lead trust, creating what investment experts call an arbitrage transaction. There will probably be a difference between the published Section 7520 rate and what the investments in the trust actually earn, and that difference creates value which will be passed to the remainder beneficiaries without estate or gift tax. Unlike the GRAT, the trust income is paid to the charity rather than the grantor. The grantor gets no income stream, but does get a charitable deduction, a benefit to his or her heirs, and supports a cause he or she believes in.

Comparison. Clients who have assets with greatly appreciated value wonder how to compare the strategies we've been examining. This is an analysis of some of the strategies already presented, compared on the basis of several important factors.

Strategy 1: Sale of Asset with No Tax Planning.

Sale of the appreciated asset and immediate payment of the capital gains tax, followed by reinvestment of the proceeds in a diversified portfolio avoids uncertainty and rigidity. It provides a going-forward investment strategy in which the cash flow and management needs of the seller are the entire focus of the management of the funds. It does so, however, at the cost of a large tax payment when the sale is made.

Comparison of Appreciated Asset Strategies

Risk vs. Strategy Matrix

Risk: Strategy:	Tax	Liquidity	Investment Diversification	Management
1. Sale/ Reinvest: No Tax Planning	Fully Taxed	Fully Liquid	Diversified but taxes due when further sales occur	Easy to Manage
2. 1031 Exchange	Deferral of Capital Gain Taxes	Not Liquid	Not Diversified	Must self-manage or hire property management
3. Family Limited Partnership	Estate Tax savings of 30 to 35%	Not Liquid	Not Diversified	Control kept by parents, who can transition to children
4. Charitable Remainder Trust	No Capital Gains Tax, charitable deductions for Income Tax	Assets are liquid inside trust, but can't be removed from trust	Diversifies Assets without Cap. Gains Tax liability within trust	Easy to manage, but payment formula doesn't change

Figure 16-2

Strategy 2: 1031 Exchange

Use of a 1031 Exchange, either by itself or in conjunction with an upREIT strategy allows deferral of capital gains, and provides diversification, but only in the real estate asset class. There can be more ease of management if a REIT is incorporated as part of the strategy because it will use professional managers. However there is no diversification into asset classes other than real estate with this strategy.

Strategy 3: Family Limited Partnership

Use of a Family Limited Partnership Estate Freeze technique can shift potential gains out of the estate of the owner and minimize estate taxes. Here, the disadvantages are the rigidity of some of these types of techniques, particularly in the face of changing estate tax laws.

Strategy 4: Charitable Remainder Trusts

Use of Charitable Trusts can provide estate tax, capital gains and income tax benefits. Charitable Trusts are most appealing for clients with an inclination toward charitable giving or a particular cause that is special to them. A Charitable Trust may provide deductions of the present value of the eventual charitable donations and is a good opportunity to diversify assets without capital gains tax on sales of the assets while within the trust.

CHAPTER 17:

Powers of Attorney, The Backup Will, Life Insurance Trusts, IRA Rescue

Chapter Contents: Health Care Issues, Financial Issues, and the Power of Attorney ▸ Safeguarding the Elderly ▸ Conservatorship ▸ Resigning as Trustee ▸ Financial Power of Attorney ▸ Springing Power of Attorney ▸ The Backup or Pourover Will ▸ Life Insurance Trust ▸ Ownership of a Policy ▸ Leveraging Your Gift Exemption ▸ Buy/Sell Insurance ▸ Insurance Contracts and the New Tontines ▸ Income in Respect of Decedent ▸ Avoiding Taxes with Your IRA

"Death is not the worst evil, but rather when we wish to die and cannot."

Attributed to Sophocles
(c. 496 BC–406 BC)

"I don't want to achieve immortality by being inducted into the Baseball Hall of Fame. I want to achieve immortality by not dying."

Attributed to Leo Durocher
(1905–1991) at age 81

Health Care Issues, Financial Issues, and the Power of Attorney.
These tools are about control of your financial or health issues during
your lifetime. Since they address management issues, there's no specific
financial or tax gain sought here. Instead, we're addressing how and
when you'll pass control of your finances or health care decisions to a
trusted person in a controlled and precise way.

The Durable Health Care Power of Attorney (DHCPOA) allows you
to determine who will make health care decisions for you when you
are no longer capable of making them for yourself. Many issues may
be contained in a DHCPOA, including long term life support, use of
organs for transplant, or whether your body can be used for medical
research after your death.

The DHCPOA is very popular in the aftermath of the Terry Schiavo
case. She languished for years while the courts and the legislature
struggled with the question of which family members had the right to
terminate her life support.

Suppose, for example, you are injured, and you can't communicate when
you're taken to the hospital. If certain kinds of treatment you might get
aren't permitted by your moral and religious beliefs, a DHCPOA can
allow you to ensure you will be treated in a way that honors your beliefs
even if you can't communicate. Since some people want to be sure that
life support isn't continued for years against their wishes and others are
content to let medical practitioners make the decision for them, I always
offer a DHCPOA when I draft an estate plan, but they're not needed by
everyone.

If you decide to use a DHCPOA, you need to choose an agent, the person
who will make your medical decisions when you can't. Spouses most

often specify each other as agent. However, if there's a reason for using someone else, or if you want to specify an alternate agent, then there are two important factors to think through: your agent needs availability and sensibility. You want someone who'll be available, at least most of the time. It's best to choose someone who lives in your town or area, and not a friend across the continent. Choose someone who's sensible and will adhere to your wishes, not a person who doesn't understand what you want and can't make a decision.

Safeguarding the Elderly. We are all aware that certain health conditions limit a person's ability to make financial decisions. The California legislature has recently recognized financial abuse as one of the forms of elder abuse that is punishable as a crime. Such an illness is not just a medical problem but can become a costly legal problem if someone hasn't made any preparations. An especially subtle problem arises with certain mental disabilities, such as certain grades of Alzheimer's or dementia. The victim may seem to have the capacity to understand a financial transaction, but this appearance is deceptive.

In one case, a lender was accused of financial elder abuse. Grandpa took out a first, then a second mortgage on his house and gave the money to a confidence trickster who fled the jurisdiction. The lender had no idea that Grandpa had any illness or disability. He seemed to be following everything, and his polite demeanor made the lender and escrow agent think he knew what was going on.

When he was later asked what happened, Grandpa had no recollection of the loans. He testified during his deposition that he had never borrowed against his house, and that the loan documents must be forgeries. He testified very sincerely that he had never taken out a loan, much less two, even though he had signed both sets of loan documents. A competent psychologist testified that Grandpa had an advanced form of dementia, under which he had a very poor memory for recent events. The inability to remember events that just happened was especially damaging because of his politeness and attentive demeanor. He could converse in an active, lively way, and yet not remember you later that day. And unless you were an expert psychologist, you'd swear he had no mental limitation at all.

Some clients worry that their older family members will get conned into taking out a mortgage they don't need, or buy poor investments, or overpriced vacation timeshares from salesmen who take advantage of them. Suppose your grandfather is getting on in years, and you're afraid a salesman will take advantage of his good nature and sell him investments that put his financial security at risk. Can you arrange it so your grandfather can't give away his important assets? Yes, there are two effective methods you should consider.

Conservatorship. If you're concerned about a family member of yours, and there's no other choice, you may have to ask that a conservatorship be imposed. This is done by means of a court hearing, in which the court system determines whether a person can or cannot care for himself. In California, conservators may be appointed for personal care, for financial purposes, or both. The court then monitors and oversees the conservator by requiring periodic reports. This process can be expensive and time consuming. However, if it's the only way to make sure Grandpa doesn't give his house away for a series of dance lessons, it may be essential.

Resigning as Trustee. There is a simple and cheap method by which you may be able to protect an older relative and avoid having a conservatorship. If Grandpa was clever enough to have a Living Trust in place, the trust can solve this problem inexpensively and without a court hearing in two simple steps. The first step is to have Grandpa resign from being his own trustee. A successor trustee then, under the terms of the trust, takes over management of his financial affairs. The second step is to take away the checkbook, any charge cards, and record the appointment of the new trustee in any county where Grandpa owns real estate. Now Grandpa's estate has a new trustee, legally empowered to make the decisions, and Grandpa has to check in with this trustee before he spends all his money on 99 years of tango lessons or gives the house away.

The downside to resigning as trustee, when compared to a conservatorship, is that there's no court supervision of the finances. Court supervision can be an important safeguard, but may involve substantial costs. Generally, it doesn't make sense to get a conservator in smaller cases. However, if there's a risk of substantial monetary losses, and especially if there are different factions in the family, the court method may be the only way of protecting Grandpa and still ensuring peace in the family.

Financial Power of Attorney. Like the Durable Power of Attorney for Health Care, there's also a Durable Power of Attorney for Finances. There are two flavors: the limited power, designed for a particular transaction, or the general power of attorney that applies to any transaction. Some estate planners include these in their standard package of documents although relatively few people actually need one in the early stages of their life. The financial power of attorney gives your agent the power to make financial decisions or sign agreements as though you had done it.

You need a Financial DPA if you have an impending health problem that could incapacitate you at some point in time or if you are in the middle of a financial transaction and will be unavailable for a prolonged period. In such cases a financial DPA can be a good idea.

However, many of the people that already have a financial power of attorney in place probably misunderstand what it does and may have created the potential for someone to do them serious financial damage. The point of a Financial DPA is to have someone else make financial decisions for you. Despite this, many people with a power of attorney already in place keep on making their own decisions; they write their own checks, decide what to buy or keep, and make decisions about what to sell. They got the financial POA just in case they need it. Arranging your affairs this way is dangerous because the person who has the power of attorney may try to do something that conflicts with your current wishes. And if it is a general Financial POA, they can legally do so.

Springing Power of Attorney. A springing financial power of attorney, rather than an ordinary power, is what most people actually need. A springing power comes into play only if the maker loses his or her ability to make financial decisions; until that time, the maker keeps making decisions himself. It is called a springing power because it springs into effect when the doctor, chosen by the maker, certifies that there's been a change in medical conditions and that the maker is no longer up to making the financial decisions. It's designed to protect the maker if he or she suffers from a sudden, debilitating illnesses. Statistically, you probably don't need one unless you have a family history of strokes or other sudden onset mentally disabling illness. If it makes you feel better to know that you are prepared, then get the springing financial power of attorney anyway. Having one could help your peace of mind, and peace of mind is a great gauge for how well you're planning the important things in your life.

The Backup or Pourover Will. Even with a trust, you need a will. Although I've spent many pages telling you that a will is inadequate for estate planning, I'm now urging you to get a special kind of will called a backup or pourover will. It is a will, but it's not a standard will. The pourover will provides you with assurance that if any of your assets remain outside the trust upon your death, they will go where you want them to go, namely into the trust.

When could you need a pourover will? Suppose you had the very best day of your life, immediately followed by the worst. Imagine that you unexpectedly inherit a hotel. You drive by to inspect it and get killed in an automobile accident. You probably didn't do anything to make that hotel part of your trust; you didn't have time to add it to the list of assets or record a new deed showing you hold it as trustee of your trust. It's not legally in your trust, and if you died without a will, the rules for distribution of this property are the rules of intestate succession. Of course, the laws of intestate succession probably don't do what you want, so your estate plan is inadequate. To avoid this kind of problem for property that was acquired suddenly, or was somehow overlooked in the planning process, you need a pourover will as part of your overall plan.

A pourover will directs that any assets outside the trust, which would need to be probated, will be placed into the trust by the probate court. Disposition of the assets will then proceed according to the rules set forth in the trust.

Despite what you see in soap operas, few people get unexpected windfalls, gifts, or inheritances and then immediately perish. Even fewer people forget valuable assets and leave them out of their trust funding. As a result, pourover wills are rarely called into use. It's more likely that the pourover will will remain in the file and never be used.

Nonetheless, I always advise a client to have a pourover will. Preparing a pourover will is easy, and if it's done at the same time as the trust, it adds practically nothing to the cost of the plan. And in those rare cases where it's needed, the pourover will can have a dramatic, beneficial effect.

Life Insurance Trust. Liquidity needs can be gradual or sudden. Upon the death of a spouse, there can be a sudden need for large sums of cash to offset financial or tax liabilities. Or suppose a young couple with two young children has few other assets, but buys a nice house. How can they assure that their children will be able to grow up in that house and that they will have enough money to pay for the children's education? Or suppose an older couple has done well with some rental real estate they own. It has increased in value, and provides a good cash flow. They would like their children to get the property when they pass away, but they have very little cash. If there is a substantial estate tax liability when they die, can they be assured that their estate will be able to pass the real estate to their children and not have to sell it to pay taxes?

Life insurance comes in many varieties that serve many purposes, but one of the best uses is to provide liquidity in just these situations. However, if you own a substantial amount of life insurance, it will be subject to estate tax when you die. It's pretty unsettling to realize that under current law, up to 45 cents of every dollar from the life insurance will be paid to the government in taxes. In other words, if you bought a $1,000,000 policy, and it's subject to estate tax, your family gets only $550,000 from the $1,000,000 policy. To avoid estate tax on the proceeds of a life insurance policy, you must keep the insurance outside of your estate.

Ownership of a Policy. Ownership of an insurance policy is an odd thing. Most life insurance is bought by one individual, to insure his or her own life, and payable to a spouse or children. In such a case, the individual owns the policy he or she just took out. He or she can change the beneficiaries, or perhaps change other aspects of how the policy works long after the original purchase. You may state on the application for the policy that somebody else, your child, for example, owns the policy. However, since the Internal Revenue Code provides the rules that determine whether you own a life insurance policy when you die, the IRS will disregard this. You are the owner if you retain too much control over your policy. For example, if you pay all the premiums and still have the power to change beneficiaries, you own it. And if you own it, it's part of your taxable estate.

Life Insurance Trust Flow of Funds

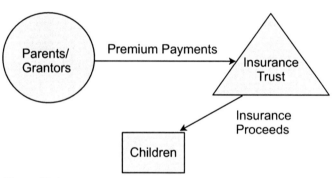

Figure 17-1

If you can prove that you really don't own a policy, then the policy stays outside your estate. That means the benefits paid to your beneficiaries when you die will not be subject to estate tax. If you wish a policy to be outside of your estate, you must take a series of specific steps: (1) You must establish an irrevocable trust, with a trustee other than yourself, and give up your ability to change or amend the policy. (2) The trust must be kept separate from your family trust. (3) The trustee must make the payments and send Crummey letters.

Since you will be the person supplying the money to pay the policy premiums, you must send funds in the amount of the premium payment to the trustee. In order to comply with the technical requirements for a life insurance trust, the trustee then sends a letter to the beneficiaries explaining that the trustee will either pay the premium on the policy, or, if they so instruct him, the trustee will send the premium payment money to them. A sample letter is provided on my website. This combination of factors puts your irrevocable trust under the conditions specified in the Crummey case and keeps the policy outside of your estate.

In *Crummey v. Commissioner* (9th Cir. 1968) 397 F.2d. 82, an appellate court ruled that this combination of factors meant the insurance was not controlled by the decedent, and therefore could be considered outside the estate of the decedent, and not subject to estate tax. This result is incredibly potent. At the tax rates in place now, a $1,000,000 policy is really worth only $550,000, and a $10,000,000 policy is really only going to net your heirs $5,500,000, unless you create and use one of these trusts. Some planners call them an ILIT (Irrevocable Life Insurance Trust) and others call them a Crummey Trust, but either way, they're not crummy at all — they're a very worthwhile tax strategy.

Leveraging Your Gift Exemption. The annual gifting amount of $13,000 mentioned in Chapter 4 is another very useful estate planning tool, and some strategies use it much more efficiently than others. A thoughtful taxpayer will consider using the annual gifting to fund their irrevocable insurance trust. A $13,000 gift each year really isn't lasting wealth, but it gets multiplied powerfully if it's used to make a premium payment on a life insurance policy. If you've got an insurance trust, instead of a few thousand dollars of gifts each year, your children or heirs could get a tax-efficient transfer of a large amount of wealth, potentially millions of dollars, upon your death.

When is an insurance trust not beneficial? If there's a fairly small amount of insurance in play and the estate is going to be so small that there won't be any estate tax, then it's not worth the trouble. Similarly, if your insurance is a group life policy, through your employer for example, it's usually not possible to implement such a trust.

Buy/Sell Insurance. You can insure someone else. It can be your spouse, a business partner, or another relative whose passage would cause you financial distress.

For example, suppose you have a business partner, and your partner's death would mean his share of the business will pass to his heirs. You'd rather not have his heirs as your new partners, so you'd like to buy his share of the business from them. The heirs typically want to be paid as soon as possible, yet seldom does a business have the cash on hand to do that.

Many businessmen purchase insurance on the lives of co-owners and write up a buy/sell agreement that specifies the steps to be taken when a partner dies. The agreement will specify how much insurance is to be held, and how it will be used to buy out the deceased partner's family.

Insurance Contracts and the New Tontines. Insurance sometimes has complicated investment concepts built into it, but at its most basic, it's a bet about death. You bet the company that you will die soon, and pay them some money to take the bet. If you lose the bet by continuing to live, that's not all bad; you get to continue enjoying your life. If you die and win the bet, however, the insurance company pays your beneficiaries as named in the policy.

Now, we get a step farther removed. Suppose you insure someone in whom you have no financial, or even emotional, interest. Pick a stranger out of a crowd and bet the insurance company he's going to die soon.

This begins to sound less like a businesslike way to provide liquidity and more like a morbid casino game.

Most insurance laws require an insurable interest to exist for you to buy a policy on someone else. In other words, the insurance regulators want you to have some definite relationship with the person you're insuring. If there is no rule about insurable interest, it raises moral questions about the propriety of gambling on human life, and whether it might, in extreme cases, encourage murder for profit!

In certain cases, insurance policies can be bought and sold after they are taken out. A viatical sale is the sale of a life insurance policy by a terminally ill patient to an investor, which is usually done so that the terminally ill patient can tap into the policy for medical treatment in advance of his or her death.

Now, in certain circumstances, life insurance can be purchased by the insured then sold to others as an investment vehicle. Stories in the media recently have brought up a new issue with life insurance for older people. For example, on March 9, 2008, the *San Jose Mercury News* carried an article on page E4, entitled "You Die, They Collect: Seniors Get Paid to Let Investors Buy Insurance On Their Lives."

In the case of some viatical contracts, the older person is contacted by investors and requested to take out a policy on himself. The policy is then sold by the older person to the investors who continue to make the payments. The *Mercury News* article includes a quote from an attorney who says "You don't want Tony Soprano buying your life insurance policy..." If insurance regulators strengthen the insurable interest rule, viatical life insurance policies may not remain an investment option for very long in the future.

Hundreds of years ago in England, tontines were formed to insure the lives of groups of 20 or 30 children for huge sums. The premiums were moderate and the payoff huge because the policy only paid off after all but one of the children died! For the last survivor, it's like winning the lottery with a twist. If you win the lottery, you get to enjoy the winnings now, over the course of your life. In the tontine, you have to outlive twenty or thirty other people to collect, and with a group of this many, the last two or three will be very elderly before they pass away. It probably isn't much of a thrill to become rich at 97. If you're really fascinated by the idea, read *The Wrong Box*, a novel co-written by Robert Louis Stevenson in 1889.

Income in Respect of a Decedent. Income in Respect of a Decedent, or IRD, is income that is received after the death of a taxpayer and after the taxpayer's final return is filed. It's not hard to see how this occurs since people seldom die on the exact date their tax return is due. Most often, the decedent's estate must file an income tax return for a partial year as well as a final return, but in certain cases, income may be received after the filing of the decedent's final income tax return. Both income tax and estate tax may be due in such a case.

Suppose, for example, the decedent is a farmer who sold crops to a buyer before he died. If the buyer pays for the crops after the farmer has died and after his final income tax return is completed, the funds are Income in Respect of a Decedent. The income may have been paid by the buyer to the estate or directly to one of the beneficiaries, but in either case, there are tax consequences.

Income in Respect of Decedent can come into play when IRA accounts are inherited.

Avoiding Taxes With Your IRA. The assets in your Individual Retirement Account ("IRA") grew in a tax-favored environment, but there may be income tax and estate tax consequences when the assets leave the IRA and come back to you or to your heirs.

It's important to understand what happens to money as it's put into an IRA. When money is put into an IRA, the taxpayer may get several tax advantages. If certain statutory rules are followed, IRA contributions are deductible from income tax when they are made. Also, any growth of the assets in an IRA account are tax deferred. Capital gains tax, which would normally be due every time an asset is sold for a profit, isn't assessed against the transactions in an IRA.

The taxpayer decides when the funds will be removed from the IRA. To put it simply, there's a tax penalty if money is removed from an IRA before age 59 1/2. Money taken out of an IRA after age 59 1/2 isn't subject to a penalty, but is subject to income tax, at ordinary income tax rates. Because most folks are in a lower tax bracket when they retire, they usually experience some tax savings by delaying the distributions from their IRA. However, there are required distributions called MRDs (minimum required distributions) that must be taken, beginning at age 70 1/2. If these MRDs aren't taken, or other circumstances mean there's too much money left in an IRA, your beneficiaries can end up paying both Income Tax and Estate Tax. Since many people aren't aware of these rules, this income may not be included in the decedent's final tax return and may become Income in Respect of a Decedent.

The effect is that both Estate Tax and Income Tax are being assessed against the IRA's funds. Because of these IRD rules, an IRA that is inherited may, in the worst case, lose as much as 2/3 of the invested funds to taxes!

To reduce these taxes, there are two potential IRA-related tools to consider. The one that exists now, but may not in the future is relatively new legislation that permits a charitable contribution of up to $100,000 to be made directly from an IRA.

Suppose you have both a savings account and an IRA, and you want some money to go to your heirs and some to a charity. If you left the IRA to your heirs, they may be forced to pay estate tax and income tax on portions of it. Instead, if you left your heirs the money from your savings and donated the IRA money directly to the charity, you avoid the IRD and Estate Tax issues. If this new legislation remains in effect and you are going to make a substantial contribution to a charity, consider doing it from your IRA.

The other tool to consider is the use of life insurance to rescue your IRA. Assume you don't need the IRA money to live on during your retirement years because you have other secure forms of income. Suppose your IRA contains half a million dollars. We've just established that if you take funds out of your IRA and pass them on to your heirs, the tax burden could be very high. Your heirs will get far less than $500,000. However, if you use the funds from the IRA to purchase life insurance, you can generate much more money to send to your heirs. Even if you're older, you can often get a single premium policy that will deliver substantial amounts of money to your heirs. While the premium may be far too steep for you to consider in normal circumstances, it may be attractive in this context. Suppose the premium to buy a new or additional million dollars in life insurance is several hundred thousand dollars. Buying the insurance with the funds from the IRA will transfer far more to your heirs than they'd get after they paid the taxes due if you left them the IRA. An IRA rescue, as it's called, works well for those who have substantial value in an IRA, don't need the funds for their retirement, and are insurable.

PART III. AVOIDING POTENTIAL LIABILITY FROM OTHER CIVIL AND TAX PROBLEMS

Lucille Ball once said the secret of living happily was "Live honestly, eat slowly, and lie about your age."

I think the secret to living happily is evaluating your financial and legal situation in light of risk and reward and making appropriate choices. The people who are happiest are aware of potential problems before they come and implement effective, well-timed defensive plans to deal with them.

In other words:
"Learn to see trouble coming, then step out of the way!"

OK, I'm not nearly as clever as Lucille Ball, but after all, I'm a lawyer.

CHAPTER 18:

Traditional Structures With Limited Safety

Chapter Contents: Protecting Your Personal Assets From Business Liabilities ▶ *DBA, Trademark, Patent, Copyright, Trade Secret, and Nondisclosure Agreements* ▶ *Let's Start A Business* ▶ *Sole Proprietorship* ▶ *Partnership*

Observer: "They haven't even been touched!"...

General Mann: "Guns – tanks – bombs – they're like toys against them."...

Forrester: "We know now that we can't beat their machines. ..."

> Gene Barry as Dr. Clayton Forrester,
> The War of the Worlds (1953)

Remember the movie "War of the Worlds," the version from the 1950s? The Martians invading Earth had bubbles of energy around their machines, so bullets, artillery, and even atomic bombs had no effect on them. This kind of shield is common in science fiction, and it's the kind of protection you want for your family's assets. The next three chapters will show you how to maximize your protection and minimize your personal risk for business liabilities and debts.

Protecting Your Personal Assets from Business Liabilities. If you own a business, you're a target. Your home, savings, and personal assets are at risk for business liabilities. And you're not just at risk for the liabilities you planned on but for unknown liabilities as well. Protecting yourself and your assets requires that you understand the nature of costly and dangerous liability traps. Then you'll understand the need for liability avoidance strategies, including how to select, form and operate business entities like corporations and LLC's.

DBA, Trademark, Patent, Copyright, Trade Secret, and Nondisclosure Agreements. There are levels of protection that you can use for your business ideas that are independent of the way the business itself is organized. These ideas, which the law sometimes calls intellectual property, are governed by a complex set of rules. Here, I'm introducing only the most basic concepts, so if protecting an idea that has value is important to you, it's worth getting professional help.

If you think up a clever name, a symbol or mark, an original idea, or a new process for your business, another person may also try to use it. If you do nothing to protect it, you have limited rights and remedies. You can try to enforce your rights as they exist under the present legal structures using statutes or laws and your rights under legal case decisions, or common law rights. You have the right to sue for damage you sustain from conversion of your property, which is the civil law term for what criminal law calls theft. You can also sue if you're harmed by misrepresentation or fraud, or if there's damage to your reputation by libel or slander. Unfortunately, the remedies available under these laws are very limited, especially if you have not taken any other steps to protect your intellectual property.

Sometimes you can use the protection of specific statutes regarding trade secret protection. However, these only apply if secret information was taken and if you can prove that you took reasonable steps to protect it. For example, if you have a list of customers or a business process in written form, make sure it has "Confidential" stamped on it and that you limit access to it.

Filing and publishing a fictitious business name statement (sometimes called a "DBA" for "doing business as") is done if you use any name but your own in connection with the business. The DBA statement is a very short form identifying the owner and the business name, filed with the county clerk, and published in the newspaper. DBA filing gives you some protection for your business name. It's relatively inexpensive, but the protection it gives is limited and applies just for your locality. Also, it's not the only system at work that regulates business names. Business names are regulated by at least four legal systems which don't always work well together: the DBA system, corporate name registration, trademark laws, and internet domain name registration. If you want to control your name, you need to make sure you register it properly in each of the systems that applies to what you're trying to protect and, if necessary, in all of them.

No matter what business form you use, if you want more protection for your name or symbol, you may want to register it with the federal or state trademark system. The process of applying for a trademark requires first that you research the official records to see that there is no one else already using that name or symbol. Then you file an application showing what the name or symbol is and pay a fee. The trademark officials will respond to your application and tell you if they agree that your name or symbol can be registered. If it is original and meets the various requirements of the trademark law, you may secure exclusive rights to the name or symbol, now called your trademark. Then you can prevent others from using it through the statutory remedies granted by the trademark laws. These remedies are much broader and more potent than the legal system's general tort remedies.

In a general sense, Patent and Copyright laws work similarly through a registration system and application process. If you comply with the steps required by these laws, you can protect your inventions or processes and your written or artistic work using the additional remedies afforded by those statutes.

If you require your employees or other businesses or individuals you work with to sign nondisclosure agreements, you can also control some of your rights and remedies by contract.

Let's Start a Business. When you start a business, you buy tools if you need them and rent office, production or warehouse space. You probably need a computer and accounting software. Once you hire the employees and get the insurance in place, you begin to produce whatever goods or services your business creates. You have withholding, payroll tax and other requirements, including getting one of those wage and hour posters from the Bureau of Labor Standards Enforcement. You get Workman's Compensation insurance, and, while you're at it, some liability insurance, property insurance on your place of business, and insurance on vehicles used for the business. If you do business in certain geographic areas, you may have to pay local or city business tax. If you're selling things, you need to track your sales and pay state sales tax. If you want to use a name other than your own in connection with the business, you must get a DBA on file. There's really not much else, in terms of filings or documentation, that's absolutely required for doing business as a sole proprietor.

Sole Proprietorship. Whenever an individual operates a business on his own, it's a sole proprietorship. This is the simplest form of business ownership. A sole proprietor must pay income taxes on his business income through his individual income tax return. The individual and the business have no separation of assets or liabilities.

The advantage to being a sole proprietor is simplicity. The activities listed for starting a business may not seem simple, but they are the same basic tasks for any business you want to start whether structured as a sole proprietorship, partnership, or corporation.

I seldom recommend sole proprietorship to anyone as the best method for starting a business. In terms of out-of-pocket costs, it is the cheapest way to go. However, cheaper start-up costs are offset by the prospect of very high liability exposure later unless it's a very small, very safe type of operation.

The biggest problem for a sole proprietor is the lack of separation of business and personal assets and liabilities. As sole proprietor, you have unlimited personal liability to creditors of your business. This is true of all the creditors you know about, such as the bank you borrowed money from or the suppliers you ordered materials from. In addition, there are creditors to whom your liability may not be voluntary, and your exposure applies to them as well. For example, a person who is injured on the business premises, and sues for damages, is also a creditor. As the owner of a sole proprietorship, a claim against the business is also a claim against your personal assets. If we're considering the "War of the Worlds" metaphor, there's no protective bubble. If bad guys shoot at the business, they're shooting directly at the owner, because he's the only one there.

Partnership. Another commonly used structure for doing business is a partnership. A partnership is two or more individuals, or other legal entities, engaged in some kind of business. Partners share costs and profits. It's important to distinguish limited partnerships, like the Family Limited Partnership discussed in Chapter 14, from general partnerships, which are the subject of this chapter.

You should start your hypothetical general partnership with a written partnership agreement to define and regulate each party's rights and obligations. The relationship between the owners will be determined by terms of the agreement, supplemented where necessary with provisions of the California Uniform Partnership Act.

For income tax purposes, your partnership is viewed by the taxing authorities as a pass-through entity. The partnership files a tax return for informational purposes, but there is no federal tax on the partnership. Profits and losses flow through to the partners as individuals. This happens when you take the information from the partnership return and add it to the information on your own individual income tax returns. You recognize profits and losses and pay taxes from your individual returns.

Samuel Johnson, creator of one of the first dictionaries of the English language in the 1700's, described traveling by sea as cramped, cold, wet, and unsafe. He commented that a journey in a sailing ship had "all the disadvantages of going to jail, with the added possibility of drowning." General partnerships are often much the same. A general partnership has all the personal liability disadvantages of sole proprietorship, with extra costs and the added possibility of disagreements between the partners.

A general partnership is sometimes the right structure or entity to manage a business, but never if asset protection is an important concern. Some of the most bitter, expensive and wasteful litigation I've ever seen has been over partnership disputes.

If it's necessary to use a general partnership structure, take a practical approach. Spend some time finding out how compatible you are with your partners before you commit to a partnership, have a written partnership agreement, and consider carefully how you will later resolve disputes that arise. My advice to anyone going into a general partnership is to have an exit strategy thought out, even before you enter the business!

CHAPTER 19:

Advanced Structures With Limited Liability

Chapter Contents: The Corporation and the Protective Bubble: the Limited Liability Concept ▶ *Let's Start a Corporation* ▶ *Corporate Roles* ▶ *Subchapter S Status* ▶ *Limited Liability in a Corporate Structure* ▶ *The Corporate Veil* ▶ *Inadequate Capitalization* ▶ *Disregard of Corporate Formalities* ▶ *Successor Liability* ▶ *Issuance of Shares* ▶ *Limited Partnerships* ▶ *Extra Protection Through Multiple Structures* ▶ *Limited Liability Companies* ▶ *Do You Guarantee the Corporation's Debt?* ▶ *Extreme Protection — Going Offshore*

"I hope that we shall crush ... the aristocracy of our monied corporations, which dare already to challenge our government to a trial of strength, and bid defiance to the laws of our country."
Thomas Jefferson (1743–1826)

"The limited liability corporation is the greatest single invention of modern times."
Nicholas Murray Butler (1862–1947)

The Corporation and the Protective Bubble: the Limited Liability Concept. There's no single best answer to all estate planning questions, and there's no single best form of business organization for all purposes. Corporations have some significant advantages for your business, but they have some potential drawbacks as well. Corporations are familiar and long-established as a legal vehicle, and they have a well-deserved reputation for safety if correctly implemented. On the other hand, corporations may be expensive and rigid and may not be tax-efficient for smaller businesses. The most important attribute of a corporation is that it allows existing owners of the business, and potential new investors, to be liable for no more than the amount they have invested in the business. This is completely unlike general partnerships or sole proprietorships.

Let's Start a Corporation. As you start up your corporation, the investors purchase shares in the company to provide the initial capital. Your corporation has rules for itself, in the form of corporate bylaws. It has its own bank accounts and its own assets. As part of the process of setup, your corporation reserves a name for itself and files its articles of incorporation with the Secretary of State. The corporation has a first meeting to approve bylaws and should keep minutes, or written records, of all corporate meetings. The corporation applies for Federal and State tax identification numbers. It must also take steps to comply with various requirements for record keeping that any business with employees needs, just like the sole proprietorship or partnership. The corporation gets and displays a wage and hours poster and gets Workman's Compensation Insurance. The corporation leases or buys some property for the business to operate from and gets property insurance and liability insurance, too. Your new corporation probably needs to get a Sales Tax Permit from the state Board of Equalization and a city business license. This is the general flow of the startup process in a small corporate setting. Of course, this is just a hypothetical business, and business operations in specific industries or areas require additional licenses and have other tax and organizational questions.

Corporate Roles. There are three types of roles in your new corporation: the shareholders, who own the business, the Board of Directors, elected by the shareholders, and the officers, such as the President and Vice President, who, together with the employees, run the day to day affairs of the company.

If you are a shareholder, your involvement in the business is very limited. You elect the directors and approve extraordinary matters such as altering the share structure of the corporation itself or winding up the company. If you are a director, you're responsible for oversight from a high level, and choose officers to hire the employees and manage the day-to-day affairs. If you're an officer you're in charge of the day-to-day operations and running of the corporation's business.

For tax purposes, your corporation pays corporate income tax and files a corporate return. It pays salaries to the officers and employees. The salaries paid to the officers and employees are an expense of doing business to the corporation, so the corporation gets a deduction for this expense from its corporate income tax. Of course, as an individual, the officer or employee pays personal income taxes on his or her salary. If the corporation is profitable, distributions will be made to shareholders in the form of dividends. Dividends are a portion of the net profit of the corporation after all taxes have been paid, but those earnings get taxed twice, first when the corporation earned the income and again when received by the shareholders. This double taxation of dividends is one of the more serious drawbacks of the corporate operating form.

Subchapter S Status. In many respects the Subchapter S corporation is a good compromise between a sole proprietorship or partnership and a corporate form of doing business. In order to elect Subchapter S status a Federal notice must be filed, usually at the inception of the corporation's existence. By selecting Subchapter S, the corporation becomes a conduit or passthrough for profits and losses. The corporation essentially elects to be taxed like a partnership with the income and expenses of the Subchapter S corporation reported on an informational tax return at the corporate level. However, the earnings of the Subchapter S corporation are only taxed at the individual level, just like a general partnership. That way, double taxation of the profits is avoided.

There are a number of technical restrictions which must be met to obtain Subchapter S treatment. The corporation must be a domestic corporation with no more than 100 shareholders and have only a single class of stock. Because of these, and other technical restrictions, companies that are positioning themselves to go public do not remain Subchapter S entities. Subchapter S status is a significant tax advantage while companies are private and small.

Limited Liability in a Corporate Structure. The most important aspect of the corporate structure is that, if certain formal steps are followed, individual shareholders have limited personal liability.

Think of the corporation as an artificial person with the ability to hold property and maintain a position as a party in lawsuits. The corporation, not the individual shareholder, has its own rights at stake and wins or loses accordingly. If a Fortune 500 company agrees to borrow money to buy a building, for example, it's a corporate asset. No one would expect that the shareholders each own a room, and they aren't obligated to pay off the loan if the company doesn't. The only financial risk the shareholders have is the value of their shares.

In order to keep the corporation alive, a good paper trail is required. The corporation must be kept legally distinct from the individual investors. Formal compliance with certain statutory rules is crucial in order to get the limited liability protection the corporation was designed to provide. Your corporation must have meetings between shareholders or directors as specified in the bylaws, and must keep minutes, which are written records of those meetings. There must also be careful separation of the corporation's assets from the owners' individual assets. Some formal procedures make practical sense, but other procedures make no more sense than a ritual or incantation. However, following these formal procedures is essential to getting and keeping personal protection from corporate liabilities as a business owner. That idea alone should make a few rituals and incantations a lot more palatable.

The Corporate Veil. The corporate structure has been abused in the past, and the law has adapted to prevent these abuses now. If a corporation fails to act appropriately, it won't provide the shareholders with limited liability. Courts refer to piercing the corporate veil, a poetic term for an ugly result. Piercing the corporate veil happens when a court holds that individuals are personally liable for corporate obligations, because of some serious problem with the corporation's viability. The court will impose alter ego liability on the individuals, because legal distinction between the individual and the corporation was breached.

Inadequate Capitalization. There's no precise minimum amount of money that the law specifies must be invested in a corporation when it's started. Owners of small corporations may lend money to their corporation in addition to buying shares, but for this purpose loans don't count as capitalization. The amount of capital which must be contributed depends on the type of business to be undertaken. If capitalization is inadequate in the court's opinion, however, personal liability gets imposed on the owners.

Example: Taxi cab company owners in a large city decided to incorporate to avoid personal liability to the owners in the event of any accidents caused by the drivers. Each individual cab was owned by a separate corporation with one dollar of capital contributed. The reasoning of the owners was simple: When an accident happens, the claimant could get only the capital in that one particular taxicab corporation, so the risk to the owners of the business was limited to the value of the taxicab and one dollar. Courts had no trouble ruling that this was an inadequate amount of capital with which to run the companies. The corporate entities were disregarded, and the shareholders were held personally liable for damages from accidents.

Disregard of Corporate Formalities. Corporate formalities are the formal acts performed to treat the corporation as distinct from it's individual owners. Although many of the formalities are small, failing to observe them may allow the corporate veil to be pierced.

At all times, corporate business must be done in the corporate name. Don't refer to the other participants in a corporation as partners rather than shareholders. Be sure that it's clear that you are acting for the corporation. Contracts should always be made in the corporation's name, and signed by an officer of the corporation:

Our Corporation's Name

By: _____

Mr. X, President

Although it seems almost childishly formal, it is necessary if you are to remain protected.

Example: An individual negotiated a lease to rent a house. He negotiated without ever mentioning a corporate name and signed the agreement in his own name. Later, when there's a default on the lease, he told the landlord that the lease was a corporate obligation of his company, not his personal obligation. The landlord sued, and successfully asked the court to impose personal liability on the individual because there was no respect of the artificial person of the corporation by the owner. Had the individual negotiated in the corporation's name, signed the agreement as a corporate officer, and treated the corporation as an entity apart from himself, the result would have been different.

Successor Liability. When a corporation gets into trouble and the owners take assets out, the court may disregard the corporation. This is often referred to as downstream or successor liability.

Example: Suppose that the business is about to fail. The owners take some of the assets that still have value, but leave the liabilities behind. They open a new business, down the street, as a corporation. It has a similar name and all the important assets of the failing business but none of the liabilities. Creditors are told they must deal with the old corporation which has no assets left. Under the legal doctrine of successor liability, the court may hold the new company and the owners liable for the old company's debt.

If your corporate business is in fiscal trouble, with more creditors than assets, be careful to respect the corporate form. If you want to use some of the assets in another business venture, document that your new business paid a fair price for the assets and don't take too many of them. If you take the name, product, and relationship with key vendors, a court will be likely to find the new corporation liable under the successor liability doctrine.

Issuance of Shares. This area of law contains many highly technical requirements and should be done with competent legal counsel. Selling an investor an interest in a corporation requires the sale of stock which the law calls the issuance of a security. To protect the investing public, complex and very technical federal and state laws regulate the sales of shares. In fact, even offers to buy or sell shares, as well as completed sales, are regulated by these laws.

For corporations that offer shares to the public, there are a series of complex and expensive steps that must be taken before shares can be offered for sale. Securities laws require that full disclosure must be made to a prospective investor, and registration or qualification of the transaction with appropriate governmental authorities must occur prior to any offer or sale of securities. Compliance with securities laws requires disclosure of copious amounts of information in a prospectus in highly regulated format. These requirements are very expensive and time-consuming.

A small mom and pop company, unlike Microsoft or GM, does not usually have to meet all of these requirements. It's simpler to sell stock in small corporations because of exemptions to securities laws. To fit within the exemptions, small companies can't sell shares to the general public, and buyers must be financially sophisticated within the standards set out in the securities statutes and regulations. Again, appropriate legal guidance is important.

Limited Partnerships. Limited partnerships are a cross between a corporation and a general partnership. There must be at least one general partner and at least one limited partner. General partners actively operate the partnership's business. Limited partners are investors who contribute money or property for limited partnership shares. As long as they're not active in the business affairs of the partnership, limited partners are protected from personal liability by this structure. To that extent, a limited partner is just like a shareholder in a corporation. There are local laws which govern partnership formation in each state; however, some states, like California, have similar laws by virtue of adopting the Uniform Limited Partnership Act, which is part of the Corporations Code. You must determine which specific provisions apply to any state in which you form and operate a partnership.

For tax purposes, general partners and limited partners are usually treated similarly. Partners agree on how profits, losses, and other tax benefits are to be treated among the participants in the partnership agreement. Income, gains and losses of the partnership pass to each of them and affect their individual income taxes. If the limited partnership was properly established and operated, a limited partner should be liable only to the extent of his investment, but the general partners are personally responsible for the partnership obligations.

Extra Protection Through Multiple Structures. If you own several different assets, you may be best protected by creating separate entities to hold each of them. That way, if you have a problem with one of the assets it will not affect the others.

For example, if you own several apartment buildings, incorporating and operating them separately may mean that someone injured in one of the apartment buildings has only the assets of that operating corporation to look to in the event of a judgment. If all of the buildings are held by the same corporation or limited partnership, all of the assets would be exposed to the judgment. You can also create layers of entities for extra protection. For example, a limited partnership needs to have at least

189

one general partner, but the general partner needn't be an individual. You could form a limited partnership with a corporation serving as the general partner. While creating additional entities adds cost from a legal and accounting perspective, it may be justified by the extra layer of liability and asset protection.

Limited Liability Companies. Limited Liability Companies, or LLCs, resemble simplified corporations. There are fewer formalities than those required by a standard corporation. LLCs have members, rather than shareholders, and are either managed by all of the members or by a single managing member. The investors are usually taxed like a partnership. Taxing the LLC like a partnership means that as long as all profits are distributed by year end, there are no taxes due from the LLC itself. Only an informational return is filed by the LLC. Taxes are reported and paid at the individual level. An LLC may elect to be taxed like a corporation if they so desire. There is sometimes a small tax penalty in the form of a state excise tax on profits of an LLC, but if simplicity and safety are both important, an LLC is a good choice for an operating entity.

Do You Guarantee the Corporation's Debt? Assume you have a brand new corporation, or other limited liability structure, with no established track record. What if the corporation uses up the money it borrowed from the bank and later can't repay it? Or if it signs a lease and later defaults on the rent? The bank, landlord, or other creditor has a loan agreement or other contract with the corporation. Without piercing the corporate veil, the creditor can look for repayment only through the corporation's assets.

Since many creditors are aware of this, to protect themselves when entering a lease, loan or other contract with a corporation, creditors may require the corporation's owners to sign a personal guarantee. A guarantee agreement provides the creditor access to the assets of the guarantors, as well as those of the corporation. Whether you should sign a guarantee for your small corporation is a cost-benefit question. The answer requires you to balance how badly the corporation needs the loan or lease in question, whether there are alternatives, and the degree of likelihood the corporation might default.

Extreme Protection – Going Offshore. If you're about to embark on a truly risky business venture, you may be considering an asset protection trust with an overseas company, or taking your assets offshore. Many clients ask about this type of structure, but after some investigation few actually do it.

There can be tremendous tax advantages to operating a company's headquarters in the Isle of Man, the Cayman or Solomon Islands, or another tax haven. The difference in tax rates between these tax haven countries and the tax laws of the United States is dramatic. If this fits your situation, these might be excellent headquarters. However, few companies have truly global interests and are able to locate anywhere. You can't simply take your business and pretend that it is headquartered overseas if it's really a local operation. Going offshore to avoid paying taxes from operations within the U.S., or to avoid fines or penalties from governmental units won't work. The government has the power to jail you as well as fine you. Being in jail does save money because jails provide food, shelter, and a wardrobe. On balance, though, I'd advise any client against going to jail just to save on living expenses.

Another alternative for a risky new business venture is an offshore trust in a remote jurisdiction. Many small countries have complex, arcane legal systems, which are impossible for a small creditor to successfully navigate. As a practical matter, you may become judgment proof if your assets are in an offshore trust.

There are significant problems with this type of strategy. The expense of setting up the trust can be high. If there are existing creditors to whom you owe money when you set up the trust, transferring funds offshore may be illegal and constitute a fraudulent conveyance.

The biggest problem with this strategy, however, is the weird lifestyle a person must adopt to make it work. Your assets must remain outside your name, controlled through an offshore entity in a remote locale. As soon as you have control over an asset located here, it is open for attachment by a creditor. As soon as any real threat of litigation appears, an offshore trustee or protector steps in. The trustee or protector refuses to distribute any further money to you, so the creditors get nothing. Because no property or asset is ever in the your own name, it's an extreme, uncomfortable, and weird way to live, and if you're in financial difficulties you may lose access to your own money.

CHAPTER 20:

Staying Safe With Litigation Avoidance

Chapter Contents: Avoiding Litigation ▶ *Alternatives to Litigation* ▶ *Alternative Dispute Resolution* ▶ *Mediation* ▶ *Arbitration* ▶ *How to Deal With People Who Owe You Money* ▶ *Understanding Workouts* ▶ *Using Available Information Wisely* ▶ *Bankruptcy and You*

"Discourage litigation. ... Persuade your neighbors to compromise whenever you can. Point out to them how the nominal winner is often a real loser — in fees, expenses and waste of time. As a peacemaker, the lawyer has a superior opportunity to be a good man. There will still be business enough."
Abraham Lincoln (1809–1865)

"I don't know as I want a lawyer to tell me what I cannot do. I hire him to tell me how to do what I want to do."
John Pierpont Morgan (1837–1913)

Avoiding Litigation. Ernie Gann, author of *The High and the Mighty*, said the life of an airline pilot was "hours and hours of sheer boredom, interspersed with seconds of sheer terror." From a lawyer's perspective, trials are like that. They are a challenging collision of abstract legal issues with real-life unpredictability. Many unexpected things can happen during a trial, and the adversarial nature of the process always tests the participants' intellect, mettle, and nerves.

Some parties are fiercely determined to see litigation through to its end out of determination or feelings of righteousness. They'll keep going through the process of preparation, trial, and appeal. Eventually, they either feel justice was done, they run out of money or stamina, or they reach a point of resignation where they are willing to live with the results. That's usually when a case ends, but it's an emotional, not a rational decision. Making rational decisions is critical to coping realistically with litigation related issues.

I always try to keep my clients out of court. I always encourage litigation alternatives such as negotiation, mediation or other strategies with my clients, but sometimes litigation can't be avoided. You shouldn't avoid litigation because you fear that trial outcomes are really the result of craziness or corruption. Although we sometimes see absurd results in highly publicized cases, good sense most often prevails. Sometimes, though, it doesn't, and the downside can be catastrophic.

Currently, most parties settle their lawsuits rather than go to trial. Why settle? Settling disputes instead of litigating them allows the parties to regain control over important issues. Imagine you're a party to a trial in which the key issue is crucial to you. The final result will come from a stranger or a group of them. The judge or jury, who are the decision-makers, listen to your side of the story and the version your opponent tells, and then they decide your fate. You can't bargain with them, plead with them, or command them. You don't know whether your arguments are working, whether they're persuasive, or whether the judge and jury actually understand your reasons. If you don't persuade them, you lose. Your may then choose to appeal and continue to live with uncertainty and expense. This is a sobering thought.

In a perfect world, cases would be decided by people who understood the complex issues and the arguments involved. This isn't a perfect world. There's always a strong element of uncertainty in trials, and it's so strong that lawyers and judges in the courthouse hallway refer to going to trial as "rolling the dice." Trials are risky and avoiding litigation if you can, is almost always the better alternative.

Alternatives to Litigation.

> "Agree, for the law is costly."
> William Camden (1551–1623)

> "Better and safer is an assured peace than a victory hoped for. The one is in your own power, the other is in the hands of the gods"
> Titus Livius (Livy) (59 B.C.–A.D. 17)

Alternative Dispute Resolution. Alternative Dispute Resolution, or ADR, is the use of alternatives to the typical court system to resolve disputes. The two primary alternatives to litigation are mediation, which is not binding, or arbitration, which generally is binding. There are advantages and disadvantages to each.

Mediation. In mediation, the mediator is a neutral person agreed to, jointly, by the parties. The mediator will hear an informal presentation of evidence and argument, either together or in separate sessions, with opposing parties. He will indicate the result likely to be reached in a typical trial, and try to prompt a settlement of the claim. In mediation, since the process is not binding, both parties must agree with any proposed settlement. A party who does not agree to a resolution cannot be forced to settle through mediation. If no agreement is reached, the dispute goes on.

Arbitration. Binding arbitration involves presentation of evidence and argument to a hired arbitrator, agreed to by the parties, who then decides the dispute. Although lawyers almost always pick retired judges or other very experienced lawyers as arbitrators, an intelligent person familiar with the type of business situation is also a good possibility. Arbitration resolves a case more rapidly than many court systems. Evidence is presented informally, which is much faster and easier than at a formal trial. For example, evidentiary rules in trials may require exclusion of certain records or testimony if they are hearsay or indirect evidence. If so, the evidence cannot be considered in any way by the judge or jury unless other witnesses or evidence can lay a foundation to support its trustworthiness. Many witnesses or documents must sometimes be called to support a fairly simple fact. An arbitrator could admit the evidence anyway, and if the indirect character of the evidence has any significance the arbitrator will weigh it accordingly in making his decision.

ADR has become sufficiently popular that many contracts now specify binding arbitration as the manner in which any disputes between the contracting parties must be resolved. There is a potential downside to this. Generally, you cannot appeal an arbitrator's decision for any reason, even if he or she makes a mistake. Simplicity and finality may not be what you want if there's a lot at stake. The right to formal procedures and the right to appeal may be more important.

How to Deal with People Who Owe You Money. The only debt collection firepower I can pass on to you is practical in nature. The key to dealing with debtors is communication, being sensible about your expectations, and dealing promptly with problems. Unless you are in the business of lending money, you should not let your clients use your business as their bank.

An unsecured creditor is the most common type of creditor. Such a creditor has provided services or goods to a person who is obligated to pay for them but has not yet done so. The basic remedy for an unsecured creditor in a civil dispute is to sue and obtain a judgment.

An unsecured creditor has little protection until he wins the lawsuit and receives and executes on a judgment against the debtor. In the pre-judgment part of the cycle, an unsecured creditor has a generalized right to be repaid but no power to compel a debtor to part with any particular asset. This means there's the risk that the debtor may disappear, or become insolvent, before paying.

The creditor can try to get an injunction, which is a court order, forbidding the debtor from disposing of assets until the lawsuit against the debtor is resolved, but the hurdles to getting an injunction are significant, and most injunction requests are denied. Courts are reluctant to grant injunctions, because there is a high burden for the court to oversee compliance by the debtor, and because it may cause irreparable harm to the debtor's business if improperly granted. The court can deny injunctive relief if payment of money damages, and not some unique or irreparable harm, is the only issue between the parties. The creditor can also try to get a prejudgment attachment order, but only as part of the lawsuit.

If a creditor finally prevails in his lawsuit, he does not automatically get paid. The creditor gets a judgment, which is a sheet of paper that says the debtor officially owes him money according to the court system. In the post judgment part of the cycle, an unsecured creditor's claim is still general in nature until the creditor begins the formal process of levying and attaching the debtor's assets. At that time, an unsecured creditor may start compelling a debtor to part with money or specific items of property to satisfy the debt just like a secured creditor. The debtor needs to pay a fee to the Sheriff's office, and send the Sheriff, with the appropriate information and documentation, to a place where the debtor has assets the Sheriff can seize.

Even in the pre-lawsuit phase, communication is the key to dealing with people who owe you money. The best collector I've ever known was no tough guy. He was a very sweet old gentleman, originally from Lebanon, and he was employed by a charitable hospital run by a religious order. He worked on collection of accounts receivable. He didn't make threats, talk tough or strong-arm anyone. He helped debtors figure out a realistic schedule to pay off their debt over time, and then he was amazingly persistent about contacting them and following up to make sure the payments schedule was being kept. Of course, some debtors didn't pay; some never do. Nevertheless, he had the best reputation and the best results of any collector I've ever known, to this day, and I attribute it to his communication skills.

Even commercial parties fail to be persistent, and it's usually a mistake. Some landlords have told me they put off sending notices to tenants who are late with the rent because it seems so unfriendly. This allows the troubled debtors to send money to the creditor who currently has their attention, and not pay off the nicest one. It hurts a troubled debtor more to let him get fatally behind in payments because he may never be able to catch up. If he really needs time, the creditor should encourage him to make a realistic payment plan, share it with his creditors, and follow through. Then the creditor becomes part of the debtor's ongoing plan, not someone the debtor ignores and avoids.

Understanding Workouts. Workouts, or debt restructuring plans, are highly misunderstood. They aren't about letting a financially troubled company or person off the hook for a while, as an act of pure charity.

From the creditor's standpoint, the workout has two components: First, a realistic payment plan is worked out with the debtor. Second, the creditor usually is gaining, or regaining, some advantage. Suppose the creditor is owed money, but has a problem with the underlying documentation. The creditor uses the workout negotiations to fix the documentation and solidify his position.

Remember the *Merchant of Venice*? Shylock's agreement allows him to take a 'pound of flesh' if the debtor defaults. His agreement failed, however, to mention blood. It was therefore impossible to enforce, because he couldn't take flesh without shedding any of the debtor's blood. Recently, one lender I know of faced exactly this situation. He made a loan to a hotel owner. The loan payments weren't being made, and the loan documentation gave the lender the right to foreclose on the hotel. The documents for the loan didn't mention any of the hotel's furnishings. Although the lender could foreclose on the hotel structure itself, he couldn't operate it without buying hundreds of new beds, televisions, and linen. He asked if he could buy the items, used, from the debtor. After all, if there was a foreclosure, the debtor wouldn't be operating the hotel anymore, and wouldn't need them. The debtor told the lender he'd hold a bonfire in the parking lot before he'd turn over a single towel.

A forbearance agreement was negotiated and executed. It gave the hotel operator six months of interest-only payments on favorable terms, which allowed him to get his business back on track. As part of the deal, though, the lender received the right to foreclose on the furnishings, as well as the building, if there was a further default.

Using Available Information Wisely. A final bit of collection wisdom is to use your copy machine. Once you prevail in a lawsuit and have a judgment, you still need to find assets of the debtor. Bank accounts are the very best source of liquid assets from which to collect. Willie Sutton, the holdup man, was asked why he robbed banks. He replied: "Banks is where they keep the money."

How can you locate a bank account in a debtor's name? An investigator will charge you several hundred dollars, or more, to locate bank accounts. Your attorney can conduct a judgment debtor examination and ask the debtor questions about his assets under oath, another costly process. Or you can use your copy machine and get the information for free. When a debtor sends you money by check, make a copy of the check and place it in your files. You have his account name, number, and the bank where the account is. The debtor may not have changed accounts. It's surprising how often this simple bit of detective work brings terrific results at no cost.

Bankruptcy And You. Suppose a customer of your business, or someone who owes you money, files bankruptcy. I can explain very simply what the process of bankruptcy does, and what your rights are. However, if you are contemplating filing bankruptcy yourself, that's beyond the scope of the book.

In Bankruptcy, a debtor files a petition with the Federal Bankruptcy court to start the bankruptcy proceedings. In Bankruptcy, as soon as the petition is stamped by the court clerk, an automatic stay goes into effect which temporarily stops all collection actions against the debtor. The stay forbids a creditor from sending a threatening letter about a debt, filing a lawsuit, or enforcing a judgment against the debtor.

My advice in dealing with someone who's just filed a bankruptcy case is to take the smile test. Anything you, as a creditor, contemplate doing to the debtor, or his assets, that would make you smile is probably a violation of the automatic stay. It doesn't mean you'll never get any payment, but the Bankruptcy court is now in charge of the outcome.

In general, there are two kinds of bankruptcy proceedings. A Chapter 7 proceeding is a liquidation, in which the assets of a debtor are gathered, certain items are preserved for the debtor, and the rest are divided among the creditors. The other type, called Chapter 11 or 13, is a reorganization. Broadly speaking, in reorganization proceedings, the debtor will continue to operate his business and will repay certain debts. The creditor may ask for additional time or revised terms on which to repay the debts.

There are also different kinds of creditors with very different rights under Bankruptcy law. If there are assets to distribute, the highest priority creditors get paid first. High priority creditors include the government for any unpaid taxes, the attorneys representing the debtor, and workers who are owed wages. Many times there is nothing left after the priority creditors are paid.

After the priority creditors listed above, there are at least three positions the remaining creditors can occupy. Creditors are secured if an asset was pledged as collateral for the loan or debt to them. Creditors who are secured are in a far better position than unsecured creditors. For example, a pawnshop owner can be a secured creditor. If he lent money to the debtor, and holds some property of the debtor as collateral, he has the right to sell the collateral and be repaid out of the proceeds. Other secured creditors include banks that have mortgages or deeds of trust on real estate and secured lenders who lend against equipment, inventory, or other assets of a debtor.

Another general category of well-protected creditors are those who obtain personal guarantees. If the person or company issuing the guarantee is not also in bankruptcy, the creditor may be able to collect the debt directly from the guarantor, outside of the bankruptcy system.

The third group is unsecured creditors. Someone who is owed money by the debtor but has no collateral or personal guarantee is an unsecured creditor. As such, the unsecured creditor is in the lowest positions in terms of when, and if, he'll be repaid by the debtor.

CHAPTER 21:

Scams, and How To Avoid Them

Chapter Content: Internet Based Scams ▶ You Have Already Won! ▶ Pyramids and Condominiums ▶ The False Balance Sheet and Tax Return ▶ No Taxes Ever! ▶ The Private Annuity Trust or PAT

"The secret of life is honesty and fair dealing.
If you can fake that, you've got it made."
Attributed to Groucho Marx (1890–1977)

Internet Based Scams. Right now, the internet handles about 210 billion messages a day, and web scams are, of course, on the rise. Sorry, but there is no Nigerian ambassador who needs your bank account number to be emailed to him so he can send you $10 million. And your bank probably isn't really e-mailing you that message asking to confirm your account number and password. They already know it.

If you have an e-mail account, you receive e-mails like this every day. Always be skeptical about internet information. The FBI has an anti-fraud website at *http://www.fbi.gov/majcases/fraud/fraudschemes.htm/* that lists the more common internet scams, including these and many others. I highly recommend checking it from time to time. Remember, though, most things that require no effort on your part and promise you great returns are probably too good to be true.

You Have Already Won! My favorite scams of the last few years are the mail sweepstakes. You get a card in the mail, from a company you've never heard of, that promises that "YOU HAVE ALREADY WON!" The prize is one of four possibilities: a luxury car, a condominium in an exotic location, a fur coat, or one dollar. To claim your prize, you must contact the company either by phone or mail before the deadline which is usually only a day after the card arrives in the mail. You're worried that it will be too late if you mail it, so you use the telephone number listed on the card to call and claim your prize.

The cost of the telephone call will be charged to you, at about $7.00 per minute. You'll probably be put on hold for about 6 minutes. Finding out that you won a dollar costs around forty dollars. According to newspaper accounts, the authorities shut down one such operation after it allegedly grossed around $100,000,000 in a year. One victim ran up $4,000 in telephone calls to the sweepstakes company because she just was sure each new card must be the big winner. Many states, including California, now regulate such contests by statute.

Reading the postcard carefully should have been enough warning to avoid this scam. Fine print on the postcard stated how much the phone calls would cost per minute and also revealed that the chances of winning were one in five million. Since only 200,000 cards were mailed out in any one contest, statistically, the chances of winning anything, other than one dollar, are almost exactly the same as the chance of having a really good snowball fight in hell.

Pyramids and Condominiums. A popular scam that originated in the Hong Kong real estate market can be played here too, if there's ever a recovery in real estate prices. Land in Hong Kong is scarce, so developments tend to be high-rise. In a new 50-story building, condominiums are sold floor-by-floor as interior construction is finished. A group of confidence tricksters buy four or five units, and immediately sell them to other members of the group for a very high price. Those buyers re-sell to others in the group. The word soon spreads that these condominiums are the hottest investment in town. As more of the units became available, prices skyrocket, because the group continues to sell properties back and forth with their own members at higher and higher prices. When the fever is at its highest, the con men sell out to frenzied latecomers at a great profit. Of course, the market really doesn't support the high prices paid by the last purchasers, and the prices collapse once the group moves on. How could the purchasers have protected themselves, and more importantly, how can you protect yourself? Use your team members. A good, independent appraiser would be the best place to turn, and your lawyer or accountant probably knows one.

The False Balance Sheet and Tax Return. A Certified Public Accountant friend of mine told me about this phony tax return scam. He was asked by a new client to prepare a compilation, or pro-forma, financial statement for his business, and a personal tax return for him. An audited financial statement requires the CPA to independently verify certain items on the financial statement. However, a compilation is based on what a CPA is told by the client, not what the CPA investigates. A compilation is much cheaper to produce than an audited set of financial statements and is appropriate in many business transactions because the CPA is standing behind the format and the math, not the contents of a compilation.

A few weeks after the work had been completed, the client returned. He told the CPA he was applying for another loan and needed another financial statement and tax return, but one showing less income. The CPA was surprised, and told the client correcting errors in the financial statement wouldn't take much time, but he'd need to amend the prior tax return not just create a new one. The new client said there was no need to amend the return; he wanted a new one. He said he hadn't actually filed the other return. The CPA realized that the client was using the tax return as backup for an inflated financial statement to make it look real.

Suppose a con man wants to trick an investor or bank into making a loan that the con man doesn't qualify for because of insufficient income. It isn't difficult for a con man to make up a phony financial statement that overstates income, and unless it's audited, there's no real proof that there's that much income. Without more information, a lender would be foolish to rely on an unaudited financial statement. What makes a lender trust an unaudited financial statement is the concurrent tax return showing the very same amount of income. A person won't normally overstate the income on a tax return; he'd be paying taxes on more income than he makes. If he's dishonest, he'll report less income than he made, not more. That is, unless the con man never files the return. The phony tax return exists just so the lender can see it along with the financial statement. The lender thinks the con man really made at least as much income as the tax return shows, and makes the loan. Don't rely too heavily on a tax return backing up somebody's financial statement unless they can prove to you that it actually was received by the IRS.

No Taxes, Ever! One client went to a seminar, and came out so eager that it was hard to talk him out of trying the proposed tax strategy.

Here's the strategy: You needn't pay any taxes to the Federal Government, according to the information presented by the seminar host. You may not be a citizen of the U.S. Federal Government!

The strategy behind this theory involves section one of the 14th amendment to the Constitution, which grants certain rights to all citizens:

> "All persons born or naturalized in the United States, and subject to the jurisdiction thereof, are citizens of the United States and of the State wherein they reside. No state shall make or enforce any law which shall abridge the privileges or immunities of citizens of the United States; nor shall any State deprive any person of life, liberty, or property, without due process of law; nor deny to any person within its jurisdiction the equal protection of the laws."

From a historical perspective, this amendment was a federal enactment to prevent former confederate-state governments from disenfranchising the former slaves (and there was a kernel of historical truth to this part of the seminar host's story, at least). The conclusion proposed by the seminar was that the 14th amendment doesn't apply to anyone except freed former slaves from the Civil War. Therefore, we present-day Americans can reject our federal constitutional rights and citizenship. We can just be citizens of the state we live in. This is the part that doesn't work.

In completely unrelated legislation, the federal income tax laws give a break to certain taxpayers whose income could be taxed by both the U.S. Federal Government and by another government. For example, if a foreign citizen could theoretically be required to pay income tax on the same money in both the U.S. and his home nation, on the very same income, he could theoretically be taxed at a combined rate of over 100%. Qualifying taxpayers get exempted from some or all of their U.S. federal taxes in such a case. The seminar host told the client he could use these provisions of the tax code to claim a complete refund of all Federal taxes he was paying, even if the other government taxing him wasn't a foreign country, like France or Japan, but his home state!

Don't waste time trying to parse the Constitution to explain why legislation about the freeing of the slaves has no unintended present-day tax impact. You may safely assume scams like this cannot work, because if they did, they'd invalidate the entire federal tax system. If it worked for anyone, it would work for everyone, and no one would ever pay taxes again. Tax court judges have little sense of humor about lame trickery. In fact, a person who turns in a tax return based on this theory had better bring a toothbrush to the courthouse, because at the end of the hearing he's probably not going to go straight home.

The Private Annuity Trust or PAT. Strictly speaking, this isn't as much a scam as a cautionary tale about a new tax strategy. New tax strategies always need to be investigated carefully.

The Private Annuity Trust, or PAT, was the hot new strategy making the internet buzz a few years ago. It was a strategy for avoiding capital gains tax on the sale of appreciated property, and it was advertised and marketed like it was the holy grail to very tax-averse clients. Suppose you have real estate which has greatly appreciated in value. As we explored in Chapter 15, a 1031 Exchange will postpone payment of capital gains tax, but requires re-investing the proceeds only in real estate. Suppose you want greater freedom to diversify, and you don't want to take any risk of nonpayment from your buyer.

Generally, any tax payment from a transaction is due when the asset is sold. There are, however, important exceptions to this general rule for installment sales transactions. In an installment sales transaction, the taxpayer/seller doesn't get all the cash up front, but parts with the asset and takes a promissory note from the buyer, payable over a period of years. There is a downside risk to sellers that their buyer may go broke and not make the future payments, so the tax law doesn't make a seller/taxpayer in an installment sale make immediate payment of taxes on future payments. A taxpayer whose transaction meets the regulatory qualifications can pay the tax in installment payments, making appropriate partial payments of tax as he receives payments from the party buying the asset. The taxpayer/seller gets this favorable tax treatment, in part, because he doesn't get any money from the buyer to pay taxes at the start of the transaction. The very real risk of future nonpayment from the buyer makes installment tax payments necessary.

The PAT was developed to create the benefits of installment sale treatment without any risk to the seller. The buyer and seller enter into a binding contract of sale, and the buyer pays the entire purchase price for the asset up front, but does not pay it directly to the seller. Instead, the buyer pays the money into a trust, established and held for the seller's benefit. The trust invests the money and pays the seller over time.

The PAT promoters hoped this structure would provide the best of both the installment sale and 1031 Exchange. Like an installment sale, the promoters proposed that the payment of the capital gains tax from a PAT transaction was to be deferred. Taxes would be paid on an installment basis by the seller as payments were received from the trust. Like a 1031 Exchange, all sales proceeds in the PAT were invested and earning money for the seller's benefit with no immediate capital gains tax burden.

The promoters went farther: A PAT was better than a 1031 Exchange, because the proceeds in the PAT trust could be invested in any kind of investment, not just in real estate. And a PAT was better than an installment sale, because there's no risk of the buyer defaulting, since the buyer paid the entire purchase price into the trust when the sale was made.

The PAT is not a scam in the sense of being fraudulent, and some people tried it as a tax savings structure, but there was a substantial risk that the IRS might disallow it, and after about a year, they did.

A taxpayer/seller in an installment sale gets to defer paying the taxes because he doesn't get the money up front. The seller in an installment sale is at risk that the buyer may not pay all the payments due over time, so the law allows the seller not to pay the tax until he receives the payments. By contrast, in the PAT transaction, the seller faced no risk of nonpayment. At the start of the transaction the buyer paid all the money into a trust for the seller's benefit. In essence, the seller in a PAT transaction created the equivalent of a savings account. It didn't qualify for installment sale treatment because the seller chose to be paid over time from the trust fund set aside for his benefit. PATs existing as of the IRS' ruling were not automatically disallowed, but were individually scrutinized, and no new PATs are now allowed.

The lesson is to be wary. Take the time to fully understand the risks behind any plan to avoid taxes, especially new ones.

A Bit of Parting Wisdom:

"It is easy at any moment to surrender a large fortune;
to build one up is a difficult and an arduous task."
                    Titus Livius (Livy) (59 B.C.–A.D. 17).

Use the advice in this book. Be critical and careful. Keep your money where it belongs, for your business and family. Don't surrender.

About the Author:

Terry Kane shares planning information gathered over thousands of hours of client consultation, research and teaching. His professional career includes more than 25 years helping clients safeguard their families from financial danger with legal, business and wealth planning. He has a B.Sc. in Economics from the University of Santa Clara, an M.Phil in Economics from Oxford University, a J.D. from the University of Southern California, and is a Professor on the faculty of Lincoln Law School.

Glossary

A-B Trust, A-B-C Trust: Revocable or Living Trust used to maximize estate tax benefits; "A" trust usually refers to the Survivor's trust, "B" trust is the Bypass trust, and the "C" trust is the Marital trust. *See Chapter 8, How The Trust Works.*

Administration of the Estate: Winding up the affairs of a decedent including inventorying and gathering assets, giving notice to potential heirs and creditors, paying taxes and probate fees, if any, and distributing the assets. *See Chapter 5, The Probate Process.*

Administrator: A person appointed by the court to manage the finalization of an estate. *See Chapter 5, Dying Without A Plan.*

Allocating Assets: Selecting assets to be placed in different sub-parts of a trust. *See Chapter 9, Allocations of the Assets in the Subtrusts.*

Alter Ego Liability: When a court rules that individual owners of a corporation have personal liability. *See Chapter 19, The Corporate Veil; Inadequate Capitalization; Disregard of Corporate Formalities.*

Alternate Dispute Resolution or ADR: Resolving disputes through Mediation or Arbitration. *See Chapter 20, Alternatives to Litigation.*

Annual Exclusion: An amount, presently $13,000 per year, which can be given to any person by a taxpayer with no estate tax or gift tax effect. IRC Section 2503 (b). *See Chapter 4, The Gift Tax and the Estate Tax.*

Annuity Payment Method, Charitable Trust: Periodic payments from a charitable trust made in specific, predetermined amounts. IRC 664. *See Chapter 16, Types of Charitable Trusts; Annuity Versus Unitrust Payment Options.*

Appreciated Asset Strategies: Strategies, such as Family Limited Partnerships, GRATs, 1031 Exchanges, and Charitable Trusts, used to minimize tax burdens. *See Chapters 13-16, Comparison of Appreciated Asset Strategies, Figure 16-2.*

Arbitration: Resolving disputes through a neutral arbitrator who hears evidence and arguments presented by the parties and makes a binding decision. *See Chapter 20, Arbitration.*

Articles of Incorporation: Initial document filed to create a corporation. *See Chapter 19, Let's Start a Corporation.*

Asset Allocation: The best mix of investments in light of the purposes and needs of an investor. *See Chapter 2, Wealth Planning; Modern Portfolio Theory and Asset Allocation.*

Asset Classes: Groups of investments which share common characteristics. *See Chapter 2, Wealth Planning; Modern Portfolio Theory and Asset Allocation.*

Asset Management: Minimizing risk and maximizing control over investments. *See Chapter 2, Wealth Planning; Modern Portfolio Theory and Asset Allocation.*

Attorney-in-Fact or Agent: Person who handles matters for another person under authority of a Power of Attorney. *See Chapter 17, Health Care Issues, Financial Issues, and the Power Of Attorney; Financial Power of Attorney; Springing Power of Attorney.*

Automatic Stay: Prevents creditors from collecting their debts without permission from the Bankruptcy Court. Bankruptcy Code Section 362. *See Chapter 20, Bankruptcy and You.*

Glossary

Bankruptcy: Proceedings under Title 11 of the U.S. Code, which permit a person or company to reorganize or to liquidate their personal and business assets with Court supervision. *See Chapter 20, Bankruptcy and You.*

Bankruptcy Petition: The first document filed in a Bankruptcy case. *See Chapter 20, Bankruptcy and You.*

Basis: The purchase price of an asset adjusted for depreciation or expenditures for improvements when calculating capital gain or loss. IRC Section 1001. *See Chapter 15, The 1031 Exchange.*

Beneficiary: The person or persons for whose benefit the trust exists. *See Chapter 8, How The Trust Works.*

Beneficiary Designation: Instructions given by the owner to specify how life insurance and IRA assets will be transferred after the owner's death. *See Chapters 5, Non-Probate Assets; and Chapter 17, Ownership of a Policy.*

Breach of Trust: Acts by a trustee which are contrary to the terms of the trust instrument or the law of fiduciary duty. *See Chapter 11, Standards For Management; Multiple Roles; Proper Care of Trust Assets.*

Buy-Sell Insurance: A life insurance policy used to provide funds so a business can buy back shares of a deceased owner from his or her heirs. *See Chapter 17, Buy/Sell Insurance.*

Bylaws: Corporate documents which state the organizational rules for a corporation. *See Chapter 19, Let's Start a Corporation; Limited Liability in a Corporate Structure.*

Bypass Trust: A Sub-Trust funded with the amount of the Federal Estate Tax Exemption for the year the trustor dies. *See Chapter 8, The Bypass or Credit Shelter Trust.*

Capital Gains: Gains when investment assets are sold, lower than income tax or estate tax rates. Internal Revenue Code Section 1 (h) (1). *See Chapter 15, Liquidity Events and Capital Gains.*

Capitalization of Corporation: Shareholders' investment used to fund operations of a corporation. *See Chapter 19, The Corporate Veil; Inadequate Capitalization.*

Capitalization Ratio: Ratio of sales price to the rental income for investment real estate. *See Chapter 14, Valuation Discounts.*

Charitable Lead Trust: Makes periodic distributions of income to a charity, and returns the balance of the assets to the trustor's family at the termination of the trust. *See Chapter 16, Types of Charitable Trusts.*

Charitable Remainder Trust: Makes periodic distributions of income to the trustor and pays the balance to a charitable organization at the end of its term. *See Chapter 16, The Charitable Remainder Trust; Types of Charitable Trusts.*

Community Property: Laws under which each spouse generally has an undivided one-half interest in property or income acquired during marriage. Arizona, California, Idaho, Louisiana, Nevada, New Mexico, Texas, Washington and Wisconsin are community property states. *See Chapter 6, Option 2: Using Ownership, or How You Hold Title to Property, as Your Estate Plan.*

Community Property with Right of Survivorship: A method of avoiding probate for spouses using right of survivorship rules. *See Chapter 6, Option 2: Using Ownership, or How You Hold Title to Property, as Your Estate Plan.*

Comparable Sales Method of Appraisal: Appraising property using information on the sales of similar properties. *See Chapter 14, Valuation Discounts.*

Conflict of Interest: A problem that arises if different parties in a single transaction have different goals. *See Chapter 3, Paying For an Older Parent's Trust.*

Conservatorship: A court supervised proceeding in which a person is appointed to be responsible for the personal or financial care of another. *See Chapter 17, Safeguarding the Elderly; Conservatorship.*

Copyright: Federal law which protects written or creative works. *See Chapter 18, DBA, Trademark, Patent, Copyright, Trade Secret, and Nondisclosure Agreements.*

Corporation: A business structure which limits owners' personal liability for business debts. *See Chapter 19, The Corporation and the Protective Bubble: the Limited Liability Concept; Let's Start a Corporation; Corporate Roles.*

Corporate Income Tax: A federal tax imposed on income at the corporate level. IRC Section 11. Some states also impose corporate income tax, although Alaska, Florida, Nevada, South Dakota, Texas, Washington and Wyoming do not. *See Chapter 19, Let's Start a Corporation; Corporate Roles; Subchapter S Status; Limited Liability in a Corporate Structure.*

Corporate Veil: The protection provided by a corporation. *See Chapter 19, The Corporate Veil; Inadequate Capitalization; Disregard of Corporate Formalities.*

Cost Method of Appraisal: Use of data about construction costs to value a property. *See Chapter 14, Valuation Discounts.*

Creditor: A person to whom a debt is owed. *See Chapter 20, How To Deal With People Who Owe You Money; Bankruptcy and You.*

Crummey Trust: An irrevocable trust used to hold life insurance or other assets so that those assets remain outside of a person's taxable estate at death.

Crummey v. Commissioner (9th Cir. 1968) 397 F.2d. 82. *See Chapter 17, Life Insurance Trust; Ownership of a Policy; Leverage Your Gift Exemption.*

DBA: Literally, Doing Business As. Statutes permit a business owner to use a fictitious name in connection with the business in a local area. *See Chapter 18, DBA, Trademark, Patent, Copyright, Trade Secret, and Nondisclosure Agreements.*

Debtor: A person who owes money to another person. *See Chapter 20, How To Deal With People Who Owe You Money; Bankruptcy and You.*

Decedent: A person who has died. *See Chapter 2, Why You Must Plan Now; Chapter 4, The Previous System; The Present System.*

Directors: Responsible for high level governance at a corporation as opposed to the day to day management of the corporation. *See Chapter 19, Corporate Roles.*

Dividend: A distribution of profits to the shareholders of a corporation. *See Chapter 19, Let's Start a Corporation; Subchapter S Status.*

Durable Power of Attorney, Financial: Allows another person to make financial decisions on behalf of the document's maker. *See Chapter 17, Financial Power of Attorney; Springing Power of Attorney.*

Durable Power of Attorney, Health Care: Allows another person to make health care and medical decisions on behalf of the document's maker. *See Chapter 17, Health Care Issues, Financial Issues, and the Power Of Attorney.*

Efficient Investment Frontier: The efficiency of an investment portfolio, relating expected returns to the level of risk taken. *See Chapter 2, Modern Portfolio Theory and Asset Allocation.*

EGTRRA: The Economic Growth and Tax Relief Reconciliation Act of 2001. Set a schedule of changes in the rates of estate tax and exemptions, phased in over a 10 year period. *See Chapter 4, The 50,000 Foot View of Wealth Related Tax Laws: Understanding EGTRRA and Beyond; Chapter 12, Changes in Assets, Changes in Laws; Planning in an Uncertain World.*

Elder Abuse: Laws to prevent physical and financial abuse aimed specifically at older citizens. *See Chapter 17, Safeguarding the Elderly.*

Employer I.D. Number: Also called EIN or Taxpayer Identification Number. Used for tracking purposes when companies, partnerships, or certain trusts file tax returns. *See Chapter 9, Tax Aspects; Chapter 18, Let's Start A Business; Chapter 19, Let's Start a Corporation.*

Estate: For tax and probate purposes, the assets of a person who dies are collectively referred to as that person's estate. IRC Section 2033. *See Chapter 4, The Gift Tax and the Estate Tax.*

Estate Freeze: A technique in which assets are transferred away from taxpayers while alive so that growth in those assets is not part of their taxable estate at death. *See Chapter 13, Estate Freeze Technique.*

Estate Planning: Passing wealth safely to your heirs according to your wishes. *See Chapter 2, Why You Must Plan Now.*

Estate Tax: Taxes imposed on the assets of a decedent, computed and paid on a Form 706 Estate Tax Return. IRC Sections 2001, 2010. *See Chapter 4, The Previous System; The Gift Tax and the Estate Tax.*

Executor: The person who is named in a will to oversee the distribution of the estate of the decedent. *See Chapter 5, The Probate Process.*

Exemption Amount: Amount exempt from Federal Estate Tax. Estates which contain less than a specified amount pay no estate tax. IRC Section 2010. *See Chapter 4, The Previous System; The Gift Tax and the Estate Tax; The Present System; Chapter 12, EGTRRA Exemptions and Tax Rates, Figure 12-1.*

Family Limited Partnership: A partnership created to manage assets and to minimize estate taxes. *See Chapter 14, The Family Limited Partnership ("FLP"); The FLP in Operation.*

Fear-and-Greed Style Investing: Using recent market trends as a basis for future investing with undue emphasis on events in the immediate past. *See Chapter 2, Wealth Planning; Modern Portfolio Theory and Asset Allocation.*

Fiduciary: The legal standard against which the acts of a trustee are measured, and under which a trustee must consider the beneficiary's interest rather than his own. *See Chapter 11, Standards For Management.*

Financial Statement, Compilation: A list of assets and liabilities for a person or business, where the format, but not the content, has been approved by an accountant. *See Chapter 21, The False Balance Sheet and Tax Return.*

Financial Statement, Audited: A list of assets and liabilities of a person or business where the contents have been subjected to testing and verification by an independent CPA. *See Chapter 21, The False Balance Sheet and Tax Return.*

FLIPCRUT: A Charitable Remainder Trust which may be converted from a NiCRUT or NIMCRUT to a standard CRUT during the life of the trust. *See Chapter 16, Types of Charitable Trusts.*

Forbearance Agreement: An agreement in which a creditor and debtor modify the payment terms or other aspects of an existing loan agreement. *See Chapter 20, Understanding Workouts.*

Funding a Trust: Changing the title of assets to reflect that they are owned by the trustee of a trust for the benefit of the trust beneficiaries. *See Chapter 9, Examples Of Funding.*

General Partner: A partner who shares in all profits and liabilities of a partnership, and has equal rights of management, with other general partners. *See Chapter 18, Partnership.*

Generation-Skipping Tax: When assets are passed down in a family in a manner that skips a potential level of beneficiaries to avoid tax liabilities, an extra tax liability may be imposed. IRC Sections 2601, 2611-13. *See Chapter 9, Tax Aspects.*

Gift Tax: A tax imposed on gifts made during the lifetime of a taxpayer. Internal Revenue Code sections 2501, 2503. *See Chapter 4, The Gift Tax and the Estate Tax.*

Gift Tax Return: A federal gift tax return on Form 709. *See Chapter 4, The Gift Tax and the Estate Tax*

Grantor: See Trustor.

Grantor Retained Annuity Trust: A trust in which property is transferred to the Trustee in exchange for fixed payments back to the grantor who created the trust. *See Chapter 13, Actual Growth and Assumed Growth.*

Grantor Retained UniTrust: A trust in which property is transferred to the Trustee in exchange for variable payments back to the grantor who created the trust, based on a percentage of the trust's assets. *See Chapter 13, Actual Growth and Assumed Growth.*

Guarantor of Debt: A person who obligates himself or herself to pay a debt owed by another person or company, thereby guarantees the debt. *See Chapter 19, Do You Guarantee the Corporation's Debt?*

Guardian: A person who will assume legal responsibility for another, typically for the underage children of a person who dies. *See Chapter 10, A Trust Should Be Personalized.*

Health Care Power of Attorney: See Durable Power of Attorney, Health Care.

Heir: Person who will inherit property from a decedent. *See Chapter 5, Dying Without A Plan.*

Income Beneficiary: A person entitled to the income created by investment assets held by a trust. *See Chapter 7, The 50,000 Foot View of the Living Trust.*

Income Method of Appraisal: Valuation of property by comparing the income generated by the property being appraised with the income generated by similar properties. *See Chapter 14, Valuation Discounts.*

Income in Respect of a Decedent, or IRD: Income received after a decedent's final tax return has been filed. Internal Revenue Code Section 691. *See Chapter 17, Income in Respect of Decedent.*

Income Tax: The federal government taxes income to individuals, corporations, and in certain circumstances, to trusts. IRC Section 1. *See Chapter 4, The 50,000 Foot View; Understanding EGTRRA and Beyond.*

Inheritance Tax: Makes the party receiving the distribution pay the tax on transfers at death. *See Chapter 4, The Previous System; The Gift Tax and the Estate Tax.*

Injunction: A court order which requires a party to perform certain acts, or forbids certain acts from being performed. *See Chapter 20, How To Deal With People Who Owe You Money.*

Installment Sales: When Buyers purchase property and make periodic payments of principal and interest over time. Sellers may get favorable tax treatment of their gains in certain circumstances. IRC Section 453. *See Chapter 21, The Private Annuity Trust or PAT.*

Insurable Interest: A personal or financial relationship with another person, required by regulators before purchasing insurance on that person's life. *See Chapter 17, Ownership of a Policy.*

Insurance Trust: An irrevocable trust which holds life insurance as its asset, so the proceeds remain outside the taxable estate of the insured. Also referred to as Crummey Trust IRC. Section 2042. *See Chapter 17, Life Insurance Trust.*

Intangible Property: Personal property which cannot be physically touched or moved, for example, a copyright, contract right, or other right to payment. *See Chapter 5, How Our Society Tracks and Transfers Legal Ownership.*

Intellectual Property: A general term for certain valuable intangible property, protected through the Copyright, Patent, and Trademark laws, as well as Trade Secrets laws, statutory Unfair Competition laws and the general common law. *See Chapter 18, DBA, Trademark, Patent, Copyright, Trade Secret, and Nondisclosure Agreements.*

Intentionally Defective Trust: A trust created with an intentional defect so that the income from the trust is taxable to the Grantor for income tax purposes but the trust assets remain outside the Grantor's taxable estate at death. IRC Section 677. *See Chapter 14, Intentionally Defective Trusts.*

Intestate: To die without an estate plan or will. *See Chapter 5, Dying Without A Plan.*

Invading Principal: When a beneficiary who is entitled to income from the trust is authorized by the trust to invade the principal assets of the trust. Often permitted only for the beneficiary's health, education, maintenance or support. *See Chapter 8, The Bypass or Credit Shelter Trust.*

Inventory: During the probate process, the assets of a decedent must be listed and valued. Probate fees, as well as certain other fees, are calculated from the inventory. *See Chapter 5, The High Cost of Dying.*

IRA or Individual Retirement Accounts: Individuals contribute funds, which are held and invested for their benefit. Income taxes are deferred while the funds are invested, and the taxpayer may be able to deduct contributions from current income for income tax purposes. IRC Section 408. *See Chapter 17, Avoiding Taxes with Your IRA.*

IRA Charitable Gifting: A technique for reducing potential tax liability by making charitable gifts directly from an IRA to a charitable organization. *See Chapter 17, Avoiding Taxes with Your IRA.*

IRA Rescue: A technique for avoiding tax liability by using the funds in an IRA to purchase life insurance. *See Chapter 17, Avoiding Taxes with Your IRA.*

Irrevocable Trust: A trust which cannot be freely revoked or amended by the trust's creator. *See Chapter 7, The 50,000 Foot View of the Living Trust; Chapter 17, Life Insurance Trust.*

Issuance of Shares: When a corporation offers new shares for sale. *See Chapter 19, Issuance of Shares.*

Joint Tenancy: Where two or more people own property and specify that the survivor is to get the property at the death of the other co-owner(s). *See Chapter 6, Option 2: Using Ownership, or How You Hold Title to Property, as Your Estate Plan.*

Judgment: A final order from a civil lawsuit. *See Chapter 20, How To Deal With People Who Owe You Money.*

Lack of Control Discount: For appraisal purposes the value of a minority share in small companies may be reduced to reflect dominance by majority shareholders and lack of control by the minority. *See Chapter 14, Valuation Discounts.*

Lack of Marketability Discount: It is often difficult to attract buyers for a minority interest in a small company, so for appraisal purposes, the value of a minority share may be reduced to reflect this lack of marketability. *See Chapter 14, Valuation Discounts.*

Laddering: Arranging trust structures or investment portfolios so that purchase or transfer of assets are made in a sequence over time rather than all at once. *See Chapter 13, Actual Growth and Assumed Growth.*

Lead Trust: See Charitable Lead Trust.

Legacy Trust: A trust set up to continue for multiple generations; used to manage and preserve significant family wealth. *See Chapter 10, Duration of the Trust.*

Life Beneficiary: A person whose rights to use assets or get income from a trust are cut off at their death. *See Chapter 9, The Roles In The Trust Structure; When Both Spouses Die.*

Life Insurance Trust: Also Crummey Trust. An irrevocable trust used to hold life insurance or other assets so that those assets remain outside of a person's taxable estate at death. *Crummey v. Commissioner* (9th Cir. 1968) 397 F.2d. 82. *See Chapter 17, Life Insurance Trust; Ownership of a Policy; Leverage Your Gift Exemption.*

Limited Liability Company: Gives the owners the same limited liability protection they would get from a corporation with fewer formalities than a corporate structure. *See Chapter 19, Limited Liability Companies.*

Limited Partner: When a partnership is made up of both General and Limited Partners, the Limited Partners have limited management and control, but enjoy limited liability, much like the shareholders in a corporation. *See Chapter 19, Limited Partnerships.*

Liquidity Event: The sale of an asset whose value has appreciated greatly, and converts significant amounts of wealth into a different form. *See Chapters 13-16, and Comparison of Appreciated Asset Strategies, Figure 16-2.*

Litigation: Resolution of disputes through formal court proceedings. *See Chapter 20, Avoiding Litigation.*

Living Trust: See Revocable Trust.

Marital deduction: Estate tax law gives transfers between spouses a beneficial tax status; transfer from husband to wife or wife to husband is not subject to estate tax. IRC section 2056. *See Chapter 8, Please Don't Waste Your Tax Exemptions.*

Marital Trust or QTIP: Sub-Trust created by a living trust after the death of the first spouse. *See Chapter 8, The QTIP or Marital Trust.*

Marketability Discount: See Lack of Marketability Discount.

Mediation: A method of resolving disputes without court involvement, by the use of a third party to facilitate settlement discussions. *See Chapter 20, Mediation.*

Modern Portfolio Theory: A strategy for creating portfolios or groups of investments based on classes of assets to maximize the investor's gains while reducing risk. *See Chapter 2, Modern Portfolio Theory and Asset Allocation.*

NICRUT, NIMCRUT: Types of Charitable Remainder Unitrusts. Used where trust assets may not produce a steady stream of cash that can be used to make yearly payments; variations on the basic charitable trust to allow extra flexibility. *See Chapter 16, Types of Charitable Trusts.*

Nondisclosure Agreements: Agreements with persons or companies that prevent or limit the party receiving confidential information from sharing it. *See Chapter 18, DBA, Trademark, Patent, Copyright, Trade Secret, and Nondisclosure Agreements.*

Officers: The president, vice president, and other officeholders of a corporation who perform day-to-day management of the company's business affairs. *See Chapter 19, Corporate Roles.*

Offshore Trust: A vehicle for holding assets in a low-tax or remote jurisdiction, such as the Cayman or Solomon Islands or the Isle of Man. *See Chapter 19, Extreme Protection – Going Offshore.*

Partnership: A form of business ownership by two or more owners. *See Chapter 18, Partnership.*

Patent: A grant of exclusive use to the creators of inventions or processes. *See Chapter 18, DBA, Trademark, Patent, Copyright, Trade Secret, and Nondisclosure Agreements.*

Personal Property: The legal classification for all tangible and intangible property except for Real Property. *See Chapter 5, How Our Society Tracks and Transfers Legal Ownership.*

Personal Representative: See Executor.

Pet Trust: A trust which is constructed so that pets are cared for as part of the final wishes of the decedent. *See Chapter 10, An Exotic Example: The Pet Trust.*

Portability of Exemption: A proposed, but not currently enacted, modification to the Estate Tax law which would allow the second spouse to die an automatic credit for any unused exemption amounts from the estate of the first deceased spouse. *See Chapter 12, Portability and Some Simple But Effective Suggestions.*

Pot Trust: A trust in which the assets of different beneficiaries may be managed as a single group of assets. *See Chapter 11, Proper Care of Trust Assets.*

Pourover Will: A will prepared as a backup device, as part of an estate plan utilizing a living trust. *See Chapter 17, The Backup or Pourover Will.*

Power of Attorney: A document which permits an agent to act in place of the maker of the document. *See Chapter 17, Health Care Issues, Financial Issues, and the Power Of Attorney; Financial Power of Attorney; Springing Power of Attorney.*

Principal and Income: See Uniform Principal and Income Act. *See Chapter 11, The Uniform Principal and Income Act.*

Priority, Claims in Bankruptcy: Order determined according to the Bankruptcy Code for repayment of creditors of a person or company that files a bankruptcy petition. *See Chapter 20, Bankruptcy and You.*

Private Annuity Trust: A tax avoidance technique discussed intensively on the internet and in print media in 2004–2005, subsequently disapproved in a revenue ruling. *See Chapter 21, The Private Annuity Trust or PAT.*

Probate: The court process which oversees the disposition of assets of a decedent. *See Chapter 5, The Probate Process.*

Prospectus: A formal document which discloses information about companies; required as part of a public stock offering. *See Chapter 19, Issuance of Shares.*

Prudent Investor Rule: Refers to the requirement that a Trustee must invest assets in a trust in accordance with an objective standard, as a prudent person would invest their own funds. *See Chapter 11, Standards For Management; Proper Care of Trust Assets.*

Pyramid Scheme: A type of investment scam in which prices for an asset are artificially inflated by trading among a group, often using funds from new investors to pay inflated returns to existing investors. *See Chapter 21, Pyramids and Condominiums.*

Qualified Domestic Trust or QDOT: When a US citizen who is married to a resident alien dies, the alien spouse does not get the marital deduction a US citizen would get unless the spouse's trust is set up as a Qualified Domestic Trust. IRC Section 2056(d), *See Chapter 11, QDOT for the Foreign National.*

Qualified Personal Residence Trust or QPRT: A trust that passes ownership in a residence from one generation to another over time. IRC Section 2702. *See Chapter 13, The QPRT.*

Qualified Terminable Interest Property trust or QTIP: See Marital Trust.

Real Estate Investment Trust or REIT: A trust which holds many properties and manages them for a large number of beneficiaries or investors. IRC Section 856. *See Chapter 15, 1031 Issues.*

Real Property: Land and any structures permanently affixed to the land. *See Chapter 5, How Our Society Tracks and Transfers Legal Ownership.*

Rebalancing Assets: As asset values change over time, the proportions of the assets held in a portfolio require periodical readjustment to retain the desired investment mix. *See Chapter 2, Wealth Planning; Modern Portfolio Theory and Asset Allocation.*

Registration: Securities laws require a registration procedure, including the creation of a prospectus, before stock is offered or sold to the public. *See Chapter 19, Issuance of Shares.*

REIT: See Real Estate Investment Trust.

Remainder Beneficiary: A beneficiary who will receive assets from a trust at the trust's termination. *See Chapter 7, The 50,000 Foot View of the Living Trust.*

Replacement Cost Appraisal Method: See Cost Method of Appraisal.

Required Minimum Distribution: At age 70 1/2 and thereafter, IRS regulations require the owner of IRA accounts to take certain distributions. *See Chapter 17, Avoiding Taxes with Your IRA.*

Revocable Trust or Living Trust: A trust which can be modified by the creator. *See Chapter 7, The 50,000 Foot View of the Living Trust; Chapter 8, How The Trust Works.*

Rule Against Perpetuities: A rule which limits the duration of trusts. *See Chapter 10, Duration of the Trust.*

Secured Creditor: A creditor to whom particular property has been pledged or promised. *See Chapter 20, How To Deal With People Who Owe You Money; Understanding Workouts; Bankruptcy and You.*

Securities Laws: Federal and State laws govern the offer and sales of securities such as stocks and bonds to the public. *See Chapter 19, Issuance of Shares.*

Self-dealing: A breach of the Trustee's fiduciary duty where a Trustee manipulates trust assets for his or her own benefit rather than that of the Beneficiaries. *See Chapter 11, Standards For Management; Multiple Roles; Proper Care of Trust Assets.*

Settlor: See Trustor.

Shareholders: The owners of a corporation. *See Chapter 19, Corporate Roles.*

Socially Responsible Investing: Investing in companies which adhere to moral or political standards and avoiding investments in companies or countries which have undesirable policies. *See Chapter 10, Investment Strategy and Controls.*

Sole Proprietorship: Individual ownership of a business with no partnership or corporate structure. *See Chapter 18, Sole Proprietorship.*

Special Needs Trust: A trust which follows certain technical rules which allow it to hold assets for the benefit of an injured or disabled person without those assets being included in the beneficiary's net worth. *See Chapter 10, A Complex Example: The Special Needs Trust.*

Spendthrift Trust: Trusts which contain a provision limiting the power of the beneficiary to sell, borrow against, or use the assets of the trust. *See Chapter 10, A Traditional Example: The Spendthrift Trust.*

Springing Power of Attorney: A power of attorney which is activated only when the maker has certain medical problems or conditions. S*ee Chapter 17, Springing Power of Attorney.*

Standard Deviation: A statistical measure whose value demonstrates the volatility in investments or investment portfolios. *See Chapter 2, Modern Portfolio Theory and Asset Allocation.*

Starker Exchange, 1031 Exchange: A capital gains tax deferral technique which permits the taxpayer to postpone paying tax on gains from an investment asset, if a similar replacement asset is purchased with the proceeds. IRC Section 1031. *See Chapter 15, The 1031 Exchange.*

Subchapter S Corporation: A small corporation which is taxed in a manner similar to a partnership. IRC Sections 1361-1369. *See Chapter 19, Subchapter S Status.*

Survivor's Trust: A Sub-Trust which is used to hold the property of a surviving spouse after the first spouse in a marriage passes away. *See Chapter 8, The Survivor's Trust.*

Tangible Personal Property: Movable items of property. *See Chapter 5, How Our Society Tracks and Transfers Legal Ownership.*

Tax Haven: Countries which attract corporations or individuals by favorable tax laws, such as the Solomon Islands, Cayman Islands, and the Isle of Man. Related Concept: Offshore Trust. *See Chapter 19, Extreme Protection – Going Offshore.*

Taxpayer Identification Number: See Employer Identification Number.

Tenancy in Common: The most common manner for two or more owners to hold title to property. *See Chapter 6, Option 2: Using Ownership, or How You Hold Title to Property, as Your Estate Plan.*

Testamentary Trust: A trust created by a will. *See Chapter 6, Option 4: What About a Will With a Testamentary Trust?*

Testator: Person who creates a will. *See Chapter 6, Option 3: How About A Simple Will?*

Tontine: A group which purchases mutual life insurance policies, with payment under the policy going to the last surviving member. *See Chapter 17, Insurance Contracts and the New Tontines.*

Trade Secret: Formulas, methods of operation, or other secret and valuable information used in commerce and protected by a system of state laws. *See Chapter 18, DBA, Trademark, Patent, Copyright, Trade Secret, and Nondisclosure Agreements.*

Trademark: A legal system of identification and registration which protects names and symbols used in commerce. There are Federal and State Trademark systems. *See Chapter 18, DBA, Trademark, Patent, Copyright, Trade Secret, and Nondisclosure Agreements.*

Trust: A legal arrangement where a trusted person, called a Trustee, manages property for the benefit of other persons, called Beneficiaries, at the request of the Trustor. *See Chapter 7 and following, The 50,000 Foot View of the Living Trust, to Chapter 11, Proper Care of Trust Assets.*

Trust Instrument: The legal document which creates the trust. May be referred to as a Trust Declaration or Trust Agreement. *See Chapter 7, The 50,000 Foot View of the Living Trust.*

Trustee: The person who holds legal title to the assets of the trust, and will oversee the trust's operation, for the benefit of the beneficiaries. *See Chapter 7, The 50,000 Foot View of the Living Trust.*

Trustor: Also Settlor or Grantor. The person or persons who create a trust. *See Chapter 7, The 50,000 Foot View of the Living Trust.*

Unified Credit: Maximum credit for lifetime and post-death transfers of property without Federal Gift Tax or Estate Tax liability. *See Chapter 8, Please Don't Waste Your Tax Exemptions.*

Uniform Principal and Income Act: A set of laws enacted in many states which regulate the treatment of cash flows in a trust as either Principal or Income. *See Chapter 11, The Uniform Principal and Income Act.*

Unlimited Exemption: No Estate taxes would be due from taxpayers with an unlimited Estate Tax exemption. *See Chapter 12, Changes in Assets, Changes in Laws.*

Unsecured Creditor: A person who is owed money by another, but has not secured the debt with a pledge of specific property of the debtor. *See Chapter 20, How To Deal With People Who Owe You Money; Understanding Workouts; Bankruptcy and You.*

Unitrust Payment Method: Periodic trust payments based on a percentage of the total assets held by the trust at the time the payment is due. *See Chapter 16, Annuity Versus Unitrust Payment Options.*

UpREIT: A strategy in which ownership in real estate is exchanged, eventually resulting in ownership of an investment trust or REIT. Related Concept: Real Estate Investment Trust. *See Chapter 15, 1031 Issues.*

Valuation Discounts: Owners of a minority interest in a small business may receive lower valuations for their shares because of the lack of marketability and control which occurs upon fragmentation of ownership. IRC Section 1001, Regulation 1.1001-1. *See Chapter 14, Valuation Discounts.*

Viatical Insurance: A transaction whereby a terminally ill patient sells his/her life insurance to an investor, and the patient can then use the proceeds from the transaction during his or her life. *See Chapter 17, Insurance Contracts and the New Tontines.*

Wealth Preservation: Keeping investments intact and growing safely, with the lowest possible income and estate tax burden. *See Chapter 2, Wealth Planning; Modern Portfolio Theory and Asset Allocation.*

Wealth Replacement: The use of life insurance to replace the value of assets given away in conjunction with a charitable trust strategy. *See Chapter 17, Leverage Your Gift Exemption.*

Will: A written document which governs the final disposition of a decedent's assets. *See Chapter 6, Option 3: How About A Simple Will?*

Workout: See Forbearance Agreement.

Index

CPSIA information can be obtained at www.ICGtesting.com
Printed in the USA
270454BV00002B/7/P